Better Homes and Gardens®

CHRISTMAS COOKING
FROM THE HEART™

TREASURED AMERICAN TRADITIONS
Better Homes and Gardens®
Family Food Collection
Des Moines, Iowa

From Our Home
to Yours

For the better part of a century, *Better Homes and Gardens* publications have been bringing American families together to celebrate Christmas with kitchen-tested recipes that reflect our country's unique heritage. Here in this special edition, we've collected the best of our Christmas recipes and their stories for you to share with your loved ones this season. It's our way of wishing you the happiest holiday ever!

Eggnog Cheesecake (recipe, page 85)

Better Homes and Gardens®

CHRISTMAS COOKING
FROM THE HEART™

Our Test Kitchen Promise

Our seal assures you that every recipe in *Christmas Cooking from the Heart* has been tested in the Better Homes and Gardens® Test Kitchen. This means that each recipe is practical and reliable, and meets our high standards of taste appeal. We guarantee your satisfaction with this book for as long as you own it.

All of us at *Better Homes and Gardens* Family Food Collection are dedicated to providing you with the information and ideas you need to create delicious foods. For more ideas, visit us at www.bhg.com. We also welcome your comments and suggestions. Write to us at: Better Homes and Gardens Family Food Collection, 1716 Locust Street, Des Moines, IA 50309-3023.

Better Homes and Gardens® Family Food Collection
Executive Editor   Joy Taylor
Art Director   Nick Crow

Christmas Cooking from the Heart
Editor   Julia Martinusen
Contributing Designer   Ernie Shelton
Contributing Photographers   Scott Little, Andy Lyons
Contributing Photo Stylists   Susan Mitchell, Susan Strelecki
Food Stylists   Jill Lust, Jennifer Peterson, Charles Worthington
Test Kitchen Consultant   Jill Moberly
Recipe Development   Marlene Brown, Shelli McConnell
Contributing Writer   Virginia Bartlett
Contributing Illustrator   Ernie Shelton
Contributing Copy Editors   Jennifer Phelps, Spectrum Communication Services
Contributing Proofreader   Gretchen Kauffman
Contributing Indexer   Elizabeth Parsons

Better Homes and Gardens® Family Food Collection
Food Editors   David Feder, Julia Martinusen, Sandra Mosley, Lois White
Associate Art Director   Shawn Roorda
Assistant Art Director   Stephanie Hunter
Editorial Assistant   Sandy Kinter

Vice President, Publishing Director   William R. Reed
Group Publisher   Maureen Ruth
Consumer Product Marketing Director   Ben Jones
Consumer Product Marketing Managers   Karrie Nelson, Steven Swanson
Business Manager   Jie Lin
Production Manager   Douglas M. Johnston
Book Production Managers   Pam Kvitne, Marjorie J. Schenkelberg
Assistant to the Publisher   Cheryl Eckert

MEREDITH PUBLISHING GROUP
Publishing Group President   Stephen M. Lacy
Magazine Group President   Jerry Kaplan
Corporate Solutions   Michael Brownstein
Creative Services   Ellen de Lathouder
Manufacturing   Bruce Heston
Consumer Marketing   Karla Jeffries
Finance and Administration   Max Runciman
Chairman and CEO   William T. Kerr
Chairman of the Executive Committee   E.T. Meredith III

Table of Contents

Pictured on the front cover:
Lady Baltimore Cake
(recipe, page 79)

Traditional Holiday Dinners

From colonial times into the 1800s, Christmas dinner as we know it didn't exist in America. Some immigrants celebrated, while others did not. Those who shared a holiday meal prepared foods that were traditional and familiar from their homelands. Every new American cook displayed ingenuity in adapting old-world recipes to ingredients found in the New World. You'll find all kinds of great-tasting examples in this chapter: a German-style stuffing with pecans and sourdough bread, a pear tart with British mincemeat, and a French bisque made with pumpkin and maple syrup. We've pulled all these holiday classics together into three distinctive American menus— choose one for your family's holiday feast this year.

Roast Stuffed Turkey *(recipe, page 15)*
with Cranberry-Pecan Stuffing *(recipe, page 17)*
Brussels Sprouts with Bacon *(recipe, page 20)*
Cranberry-Maple Sauce *(recipe, page 11)*

Ginger-Pumpkin Bisque
Prep: 40 minutes • Cook: 20 minutes

    1   cup chopped onion
    2   teaspoons grated fresh ginger
    2   tablespoons walnut oil or cooking oil
   ¼   cup all-purpose flour
    4   cups chicken broth
   ½   cup apple juice or apple cider
    1   15-ounce can pumpkin
   ⅓   cup pure maple syrup
    2   bay leaves
   ¼   teaspoon dried thyme, crushed
   ¼   teaspoon ground cinnamon
   ¼   teaspoon pepper
   ⅛   teaspoon ground cloves
    1   cup half-and-half or whipping cream
   ½   teaspoon vanilla
        Fresh thyme (optional)

1. In a 3-quart saucepan, cook and stir onion and fresh ginger in hot oil about 5 minutes or until tender.

2. Stir in flour. Carefully add broth and apple juice all at once. Cook and stir until thickened and bubbly.

3. Stir in pumpkin, maple syrup, bay leaves, thyme, cinnamon, pepper, and cloves. Bring to boiling; reduce heat. Cover and simmer for 20 minutes, stirring occasionally. Remove from heat. Cool slightly. Discard bay leaves.

4. Pour about *2 cups* of the soup mixture into blender container or food processor bowl. Cover; blend or process until smooth. Pour into bowl. Repeat until all is blended.

5. Return mixture to saucepan. Stir in half-and-half and vanilla; heat through, but do not boil. To serve, ladle into soup bowls. If desired, swirl a little additional half-and-half into each serving; garnish with fresh thyme. *Makes 8 to 10 first-course servings.*

Corn and Crab Chowder
Start to finish: 35 minutes

    3   ears fresh sweet corn or 1 cup loose-pack
          frozen whole kernel corn
    1   cup chicken broth
   ½   cup sliced green onions
   ½   cup chopped green sweet pepper
  1½   teaspoons dried fines herbes, crushed, or
          ¾ teaspoon dried basil, crushed
   ½   teaspoon ground white pepper
    3   cups milk
    3   tablespoons cornstarch
    1   6- or 6½-ounce can crabmeat, drained,
          flaked, and cartilage removed, or meat
          from 1½ pounds cooked crab legs
    6   ounces process Swiss cheese or process
          Gruyère cheese, shredded (1½ cups)

1. Cut kernels from ears of corn; scrape ears to remove milky portion (you should have about 1½ cups corn).

2. In a large saucepan, combine the fresh or frozen corn, broth, green onions, green pepper, fines herbes, and white pepper. Bring to boiling; reduce heat. Cover and simmer for 5 minutes.

3. Stir together the milk and cornstarch. Stir into the hot mixture. Cook and stir until thickened and bubbly. Stir in crabmeat and cheese; heat and stir until cheese is melted. *Makes 8 first-course servings.*

Corn and Ham Chowder: Prepare Corn and Crab Chowder as directed, except substitute 1 cup diced cooked *ham* for the crabmeat.

Ginger-Pumpkin Bisque

Oyster and Scallop Stew

Start to finish: 30 minutes

½ pound fresh or frozen bay scallops
½ pint fresh or frozen shucked oysters
  (about 6 ounces with ¼ cup liquid)
3 slices bacon, halved crosswise
¼ cup finely chopped green onions
3 cups half-and-half or light cream
2 tablespoons dry sherry or dry white wine
½ teaspoon salt
¼ teaspoon pepper
2 tablespoons snipped fresh basil

1. Thaw scallops and oysters, if frozen. Rinse scallops; pat dry. Set aside.

2. In a large saucepan, cook bacon over medium heat until crisp. Drain bacon, reserving *1 tablespoon* of the drippings in pan. Crumble bacon; set aside.

3. Cook green onions in hot drippings for 2 to 3 minutes or until tender. Add the undrained oysters. Cook, uncovered, for 3 minutes, stirring occasionally.

4. Add scallops, half-and-half, sherry, salt, and pepper. Bring mixture just to a simmer over medium heat, stirring occasionally. Cook and stir for 1 minute more or until scallops are opaque.

5. To serve, ladle into soup bowls. Sprinkle with bacon and basil. *Makes 6 first-course servings.*

Oyster and Scallop Stew

Wild Mushroom Soup

Prep: 50 minutes • Cook: 30 minutes

    1 ounce dried porcini or other dried
        mushrooms
    ½ cup boiling chicken broth
    ¼ cup dry Madeira wine
    ¼ cup chopped onion
    ½ cup butter
    1 pound fresh button mushrooms, sliced
        (about 6 cups)
    4 ounces fresh shiitake mushrooms, sliced and
        stems removed (about 1½ cups)
    ⅔ cup all-purpose flour
    8 cups chicken broth
    ½ teaspoon pepper
    1½ cups buttermilk
        Fresh chives (optional)

Wild Mushroom Soup

1. In a small bowl, combine dried mushrooms, the ½ cup broth, and the wine. Let stand for 20 minutes. Drain, discarding liquid. Coarsely chop mushrooms; set aside.

2. In a Dutch oven, cook and stir onion in hot butter for 2 to 3 minutes or until tender. Stir in soaked and fresh mushrooms; cook for 3 to 4 minutes more or until most of the liquid has evaporated. Stir in flour. Stir in the 8 cups broth and the pepper. Bring to boiling; reduce heat. Cook, uncovered, for 30 minutes, stirring occasionally.

3. If desired, remove *4 cups* of the soup mixture. Place, *half* at a time, in blender or food processor bowl; cover and blend or process until smooth. Return to saucepan. Stir in buttermilk; heat through but do not boil.

4. To serve, ladle into soup bowls. If desired, garnish with additional sliced fresh mushrooms and chives. *Makes 8 to 12 first-course servings.*

Cranberry-Maple Sauce

Start to finish: 20 minutes

    ¾ cup packed brown sugar
    ¾ cup pure maple syrup or
        maple-flavored syrup
    ⅓ cup water
    3 cups fresh cranberries (12 ounces)
    1 tablespoon finely shredded orange peel or
        lemon peel

1. In a medium saucepan, combine brown sugar, maple syrup, and water. Bring to boiling, stirring to dissolve sugar; reduce heat. Simmer, uncovered, for 2 minutes, stirring occasionally.

2. Stir in cranberries. Return to boiling; reduce heat. Simmer, uncovered, for 3 to 4 minutes or until cranberry skins pop, stirring occasionally. Remove from heat. Stir in orange peel. Serve warm or chilled. *Makes about 3 cups.*

Make-Ahead Tip: Prepare Cranberry-Maple Sauce as directed. Cover and refrigerate sauce for up to 3 days.

*B*efore the pioneers could plant their own crops, they had to gather what was available. From the Indians, they learned which mushroom varieties were good to eat. They also found that mushrooms could be dried for use throughout the holiday and winter seasons. That's why mushrooms appear in so many early American dishes, such as pot pie, stuffings, sauces, and hearty soups.

*L*et it be said: No American holiday table is complete without a bowl of glistening ruby-red cranberry sauce. Here the tangy berry is tamed by the native North American sweetener—maple syrup. Pictured on page 7.

Fig and Orange Salad

Fig and Orange Salad
Start to finish: 25 minutes

The Dutch in New Amsterdam often set out three oranges the night they waited for Saint Nicholas to arrive. The fruit symbolized the sacks of gold Saint Nicholas gave as dowries to three poor sisters. Oranges are as good as gold in this salad that tosses the juicy sections with figs, toasted pecans, and salad greens.

6 cups mesclun or mixed salad greens
3 green onions, thinly sliced
2 tablespoons olive oil
1 teaspoon finely shredded orange peel
2 tablespoons orange juice
1 tablespoon champagne vinegar or white wine vinegar
1 8- or 9-ounce package dried calimyrna figs, cut into thin wedges (about 1½ cups)
1⅓ cups orange sections (4 oranges)
   Salt
   Pepper
¼ cup pecan pieces, toasted

1. In a large salad bowl, combine salad greens and green onions.

2. For dressing, in a small bowl, whisk together olive oil, orange peel, orange juice, and vinegar. Pour dressing over greens mixture; toss gently to coat. Add figs and orange sections; toss gently to combine. Season to taste with salt and pepper.

3. To serve, arrange greens mixture on salad plates. Sprinkle with pecans. *Makes 6 servings.*

Layered Cranberry-Apple Mold
Prep: 1 hour 30 minutes • Chill: 6 hours

- 1 6-ounce package lemon-flavored gelatin
- ½ cup sugar
- 1 cup boiling water
- 1½ cups cranberry-apple drink
- 1 16-ounce can whole cranberry sauce
- 1 1.3-ounce envelope whipped dessert topping mix
- 1 large apple, cored and finely chopped (1¼ cups)
- ¼ cup mayonnaise or salad dressing
  Sugared cranberries (recipe, page 26) (optional)
  Fresh mint (optional)

1. In a medium bowl, dissolve gelatin and sugar in boiling water. Stir in cranberry-apple drink. Transfer *1¾ cups* of the mixture to another bowl; cover and chill in the refrigerator about 30 minutes or until partially set (the consistency of unbeaten egg whites). Set remaining gelatin-drink mixture aside.

2. Fold cranberry sauce into partially set gelatin-drink mixture; pour into an 8-cup ring mold or a 2-quart square dish. Cover and chill in the refrigerator about 30 minutes or until almost firm. Chill remaining gelatin-drink mixture in refrigerator about 30 minutes or until partially set (the consistency of unbeaten egg whites).

3. Meanwhile, prepare topping mix according to package directions; fold into partially set gelatin-drink mixture along with apple and mayonnaise. Spoon over chilled cranberry sauce-gelatin layer in mold or square dish. Cover and chill in the refrigerator about 6 hours or until firm.

4. If using mold, unmold gelatin salad onto platter. (For easier unmolding, set mold into a sink filled with warm water for several seconds or until gelatin separates from the mold.) If using dish, cut gelatin salad into rectangles. If desired, garnish with sugared cranberries and fresh mint. *Makes 12 servings.*

*U*nflavored gelatin in granular form was unknown until 1890, and flavored gelatin wasn't popular until the early 1900s. Before that, homemakers made their own gelatin by boiling calf's or pig's feet, or the bladders of certain fish. Think of that next time you spoon into your aunt's gelatin salad or grandma's chiffon pie.

Layered Cranberry-Apple Mold

Beet and Apple Salad

B eets were beloved by the Eastern Europeans who settled in the New World. They grew well in the colder northern climates and could be stored long into the winter. Although the Polish used beets in borscht (beet soup), the ruby-red gem soon was adapted for a variety of holiday dishes.

Beet and Apple Salad
Prep: 55 minutes • Chill: 2 hours

    3 medium beets (about 1 pound total)
          or one 16-ounce can julienne beets,
          rinsed and drained
    ⅓ cup salad oil
    ⅓ cup white wine vinegar
    2 teaspoons finely shredded orange peel
    ¼ cup orange juice
    2 green onions, sliced (¼ cup)
    2 tablespoons snipped fresh mint or
          2 teaspoons dried mint, crushed
    2 teaspoons honey
    6 cups torn romaine lettuce
    2 medium tart green apples, coarsely chopped

1. If using whole beets, in a large saucepan, combine beets and enough water to cover. Bring to boiling; reduce heat. Cover and simmer for 40 to 50 minutes or until tender; drain. Cool slightly; slip off skins and cut into thin, bite-size strips.

2. Meanwhile, for dressing, in a screw-top jar, combine salad oil, white wine vinegar, orange peel, orange juice, green onions, mint, and honey. Cover and shake well.

3. In a medium bowl, combine beet strips and ¼ *cup* of the dressing. Cover and refrigerate the beet mixture and the remaining dressing for at least 2 hours or up to 24 hours.

4. To serve, in a large bowl, combine torn romaine and chopped apples. Toss apple mixture with the remaining dressing. Using a slotted spoon, spoon beet mixture over apple mixture in bowl. *Makes 8 servings.*

Roast Stuffed Turkey

1. Measure out the amount of stuffing that will go into the bird, allowing ¾ cup per pound of bird. (That's about 11 cups for a 15-pound bird.)

2. Spoon some stuffing loosely into neck cavity. Pull the neck skin over stuffing; fasten to back with a short skewer or wooden toothpicks.

3. Unhook the legs or one of the legs, if you can't get both out. (The drumsticks are usually held in place by a band of skin or a metal or plastic clamp.) Loosely spoon stuffing into the body cavity. Don't pack it in or the stuffing may not be fully cooked by the time the turkey is done.

4. Spoon any remaining stuffing into a baking dish or casserole, and cover and refrigerate it until about an hour before the turkey is done—then bake the extra stuffing alongside the bird. (If you don't have a meat thermometer, it's safer to bake the stuffing in a casserole rather than in the turkey.) If you prefer not to stuff your turkey, place quartered onions and celery in the body cavity to add flavor to the drippings you'll be using in your gravy, then pull the neck skin to back; fasten as above.

5. Tuck the drumsticks under the band of skin that crosses the tail, or reset into the leg clamp. If there's no band or clamp, tie the drumsticks together with 100%-cotton twine (kitchen string). Twist the wing tips under the back—this gives the turkey a stable base.

6. Place the oven rack in its lowest position; preheat the oven to 325°. Place turkey, breast side up, on a rack in a shallow baking pan that has sides no deeper than about 2 inches. (Yes, supermarket foil pans work just fine.) To enhance browning, brush the bird with cooking oil. Push a meat thermometer into the center of an inside thigh muscle, not touching bone.

7. Cover turkey loosely with foil, pressing it over drumsticks and neck. Roast, using the timings in the chart below as a guide. (Most turkeys come injected with broth to keep them moist, so basting the bird during cooking is not necessary.)

8. When the turkey has been in the oven for two-thirds of the time shown on the chart, cut skin or string between drumsticks. For the last 30 to 45 minutes of roasting, remove foil to allow the skin to brown.

9. When the bird is done, the meat thermometer in the thigh should register 180° and the stuffing should be at least 165°. The drumsticks should move easily in their sockets, and the thickest parts should feel soft when pressed. The juices from the thigh should run clear when pierced deeply with a long-tined fork.

10. Remove the turkey from the oven and cover it loosely with foil. Let stand for 20 minutes. Release legs from leg clamp, if present. Remove stuffing, then carve turkey.

Note: You can keep the turkey at room temperature for up to 2 hours after it comes out of the oven. After that, refrigerate the bird and stuffing separately for up to 4 days.

Stuffed Whole Turkey Roasting Guide

Ready to Cook	Oven Temperature	Roasting Time
8 to 12 lb.	325°	3 to 3¾ hours
12 to 14 lb.	325°	3¼ to 4½ hours
14 to 18 lb.	325°	4 to 5 hours
18 to 20 lb.	325°	4½ to 5¼ hours
20 to 24 lb.	325°	4¾ to 5¾ hours

For unstuffed turkeys of the same weight, reduce the total cooking time by 15 to 45 minutes. The turkey is done when the thigh temperature reaches 180°.

MENU

American Turkey Dinner for 8

From the time of the first Thanksgiving in Plymouth, turkey has been the feast food for the American table. Pictured on page 7.

Corn and Crab Chowder (recipe, page 8)

Beet and Apple Salad (recipe opposite)

Roast Stuffed Turkey (directions at left) with Cranberry-Pecan Stuffing (recipe, page 17)

Brussels Sprouts with Bacon (recipe, page 20)

Mashed Potatoes and Parsnips (recipe, page 22)

Cranberry-Maple Sauce (recipe, page 11)

Anadama Bread (recipe, page 63)

Pear and Mincemeat Tart (recipe, page 27)

Apple-Walnut Sourdough Stuffing
Prep: 30 minutes

    2 cups chopped celery
 1¾ cups chopped onion
    ¾ teaspoon dried sage, crushed
    ½ teaspoon salt
    ½ teaspoon pepper
    ¼ teaspoon dried thyme, crushed
    3 tablespoons butter or margarine
    2 cups chopped apples
    4 cloves garlic, minced
   16 ounces day-old sourdough bread, cut into
         ¾-inch pieces (about 9½ cups)
    ¾ cup raisins
    ¾ cup walnuts or pecans, toasted and
         coarsely chopped
    ¼ cup snipped fresh Italian flat-leaf parsley
 1¾ to 2 cups chicken broth

1. In a large skillet, cook and stir celery, onion, sage, salt, pepper, and thyme in hot butter for 8 to 10 minutes or until vegetables are tender.

2. Stir in chopped apples and garlic; cook and stir for 2 to 3 minutes or until the apples begin to soften.

3. Place bread in a large bowl. Add celery mixture, raisins, walnuts, and parsley. Drizzle with enough of the chicken broth (about 1¾ cups) to moisten, tossing gently.

4. Use to stuff a 14-pound turkey (see page 15). (Or place stuffing in a greased 3-quart rectangular baking dish. If you want a moist stuffing, drizzle with the remaining chicken broth. Cover with foil. Bake in a 325° oven for 30 minutes. Remove foil and bake about 15 minutes more or until tops of bread cubes are brown.) *Makes 12 to 14 servings.*

Sausage-Corn Bread Stuffing
Prep: 30 minutes

    ¾ pound bulk pork sausage
    ¾ cup finely chopped onion
    ½ cup chopped green sweet pepper
    ½ cup chopped celery
    ½ cup butter or margarine
    5 cups dry bread cubes
 4½ cups crumbled corn bread
    ¾ cup chopped pecans, toasted (optional)
    1 teaspoon poultry seasoning
    ⅛ teaspoon ground black pepper
    1 to 1¼ cups chicken broth

1. In a large skillet, cook sausage until brown. Drain; set aside.

2. In the same skillet, cook and stir onion, green pepper, and celery in hot butter about 5 minutes or until tender; set aside.

3. In a large bowl, combine bread cubes and corn bread. Add cooked sausage, onion mixture, pecans (if desired), poultry seasoning, and black pepper. Drizzle with enough of the chicken broth (about 1 cup) to moisten, tossing gently.

4. Use to stuff an 11- to 12-pound turkey (see page 15). (Or place the stuffing in a greased 2-quart casserole. If you want a moist stuffing, drizzle with the remaining chicken broth. Cover and bake in a 325° oven for 30 to 45 minutes or until heated through.) *Makes 10 to 12 servings.*

Quick Sausage-Corn Bread Stuffing: Prepare Sausage-Corn Bread Stuffing as directed, except omit the crumbled corn bread and substitute one 8-ounce package (3 cups) *corn bread stuffing mix*. Reduce poultry seasoning to ½ teaspoon; omit black pepper. Use *water* in place of broth.

Cranberry-Pecan Stuffing
Prep: 30 minutes

1½ cups sliced celery
¾ cup chopped onion
⅓ cup butter or margarine
1½ teaspoons dried sage, crushed
¾ teaspoon dried thyme, crushed
½ teaspoon pepper
9 cups dry bread cubes
¾ cup chopped pecans or hazelnuts
¾ cup dried cranberries
¾ to 1 cup chicken broth

1. In a small saucepan, cook and stir celery and onion in hot butter about 5 minutes or until tender. Remove from heat. Stir in sage, thyme, and pepper.

2. Place bread cubes in a large bowl. Add celery mixture, pecans, and cranberries. Drizzle with enough of the chicken broth (about ¾ cup) to moisten, tossing gently.

3. Use to stuff a 16-pound turkey (see page 15). (Or place stuffing in a greased 3-quart casserole. If you want a moist stuffing, drizzle with remaining chicken broth. Cover and bake in a 325° oven about 45 minutes or until heated through.) *Makes 12 to 14 servings.*

Mushroom-Wild Rice Stuffing
Prep: 15 minutes • Cook: 45 minutes

1 cup uncooked wild rice
4 cups water
1 cup uncooked brown rice
1 tablespoon instant chicken bouillon granules
1 teaspoon salt
1 teaspoon ground nutmeg
8 cups sliced fresh mushrooms
2 cups chopped celery
1 cup chopped onion
2 cups shredded carrot

1. Rinse wild rice in a strainer under cold water about 1 minute. In a 4-quart Dutch oven, combine wild rice, the 4 cups water, the brown rice, bouillon granules, salt, and nutmeg. Bring to boiling; reduce heat. Cover and simmer for 20 minutes.

2. Stir in mushrooms, celery, and onion. Return to boiling; reduce heat to medium-low. Cover and cook about 25 minutes more or until rice is tender, stirring occasionally. Drain. Stir in carrot.

3. Use to stuff a 10- to 12-pound turkey (see page 15). (Or serve immediately.) *Makes 12 servings.*

Make-Ahead Tip: Prepare Mushroom-Wild Rice Stuffing as directed; spoon into a 3-quart casserole. Cover and refrigerate for up to 24 hours. Bake, covered, in a 325° oven for 65 to 75 minutes or until heated through.

*I*n a modern-day pairing, cranberries from the North meet pecans from the South. Dry the bread cubes the old-fashioned way by letting them stand (loosely covered) at room temperature for 8 to 12 hours. Or to speed up the drying, spread the cubes in a single layer on a baking pan and bake in a 300° oven for 10 to 15 minutes or until dry. Pictured on page 7.

*W*ild rice is a uniquely American crop. The Indians of the Great Lakes area would harvest it by canoeing through the marsh grass and beating the grain from the stalks into their canoes. In this homey dressing, the chewy texture of wild rice is accented with brown rice, nutmeg, and mushrooms.

Mushroom-Stuffed Pork Roast

Prep: 30 minutes • Roast: 1¼ hours • Stand: 15 minutes

1¾ cups chopped assorted fresh mushrooms
(such as brown, shiitake, and/or oyster)
¼ cup finely chopped onion
2 tablespoons butter or margarine
2 tablespoons fine dry bread crumbs
1 teaspoon snipped fresh thyme or sage
or ½ teaspoon dried thyme or sage, crushed
1 3- to 4-pound pork loin center rib roast, backbone loosened (6 ribs total)
1 recipe White Wine and Shallot Sauce

1. For stuffing, in a large skillet, cook mushrooms and onion in hot butter about 3 minutes or until tender. Stir in bread crumbs, thyme, ¼ teaspoon *salt,* and a dash *pepper.* Set aside.

2. Trim fat from meat. On meaty side, cut a 3½-inch-long and 1-inch-deep pocket above each rib, making 6 pockets. Spoon stuffing into pockets. Place meat, rib side down, in a shallow roasting pan. Sprinkle with *salt* and *pepper.* Insert meat thermometer into thickest part, not touching bone.

3. Roast in a 325° oven for 1¼ to 1¾ hours or until thermometer registers 155°. After 1 hour, cover loosely with foil to prevent overbrowning. Remove roast from oven. Cover with foil; let stand 15 minutes. (The meat's temperature will rise 5° during standing.) Slice roast between ribs. Serve with White Wine and Shallot Sauce. *Makes 6 servings.*

White Wine and Shallot Sauce: In a medium saucepan, stir together 1¼ cups *chicken broth;* ½ cup *dry white wine, apple juice, or apple cider;* and 2 tablespoons finely chopped *shallot.* Bring just to boiling; reduce heat. Simmer, uncovered, about 20 minutes or until reduced to 1 cup. Stir together 2 tablespoons softened *butter* and 1 tablespoon *all-purpose flour;* stir into wine mixture, *1 teaspoon* at a time, stirring constantly. Continue cooking and stirring until thickened. Cook and stir for 1 minute more. Stir in 1 teaspoon snipped *fresh thyme or sage* or ½ teaspoon *dried thyme or sage,* crushed.

Mushroom-Stuffed Pork Roast (recipe above), Red Cabbage with Fennel (recipe, page 20), and Wild Rice Pilaf (recipe, page 23)

Holiday Glazed Ham (recipe below) and
Cider-Glazed Yams with Pears (recipe, page 22)

Holiday Glazed Ham

Prep: 20 minutes • Bake: 1¼ hours

> 1 4- to 6-pound cooked boneless ham
> 1 recipe Maple-Pecan Glaze or
>   Cranberry Glaze

1. Place ham on a rack in a shallow baking pan. If desired, use a paring knife to score top of ham in a diamond pattern, making cuts ¼ inch deep. Insert meat thermometer into center.

2. Bake in a 325° oven for 1¼ to 2 hours or until thermometer registers 140°. During the last 15 minutes of baking, brush ham with Maple-Pecan Glaze or Cranberry Glaze. Heat any remaining glaze and pass with the ham. *Makes 16 to 24 servings.*

Maple-Pecan Glaze: In a small saucepan, combine 1½ cups *pure maple syrup or maple-flavored syrup* and 1½ cups *orange marmalade*. Heat and stir until bubbly. Whisk in 2 tablespoons *butter or margarine* until smooth. Stir in ¾ cup *pecan pieces,* toasted. *Makes 3 cups.*

Cranberry Glaze: In a small saucepan, combine one 12-ounce can *frozen cranberry juice concentrate,* thawed; 3 tablespoons *Dijon-style mustard;* 2 tablespoons *brown sugar;* 2 tablespoons *lemon juice;* 4 teaspoons *cornstarch;* and ¼ teaspoon *ground cloves.* Cook and stir until thickened and bubbly. Cook and stir for 2 minutes more. *Makes 1¾ cups.*

Red Cabbage with Fennel

Start to finish: 35 minutes

    4   medium fennel bulbs with leafy tops
        (about 2 pounds)
  ¾   cup apple juice or apple cider
  ¼   cup cider vinegar
    4   cloves garlic, minced
    1   teaspoon instant chicken bouillon granules
    2   tablespoons cooking oil
    2   10-ounce packages shredded red cabbage
        (about 8 cups total)
  ¼   cup packed brown sugar
  ½   teaspoon fennel seed, crushed

1. Remove upper stalks from fennel, including feathery leaves; reserve leaves and discard stalks. Discard any wilted outer layers on fennel bulbs; cut off a thin slice from base of each bulb. Quarter each fennel bulb lengthwise. Chop enough of the reserved fennel leaves to make 2 teaspoons; set aside along with a few sprigs of the feathery leaves.

2. In a small bowl, combine apple juice and vinegar. In a large saucepan, combine fennel wedges, *½ cup* of the apple juice mixture, the garlic, and bouillon granules.

Bring to boiling; reduce heat. Cover and simmer for 14 to 16 minutes or until the fennel is tender.

3. Meanwhile, pour *1 tablespoon* of the oil into a large skillet or wok. Preheat over medium-high heat. Add *1 package* of the cabbage; stir-fry for 3 to 5 minutes or until crisp-tender. Transfer cooked cabbage to a bowl; cover and keep warm. Repeat with the remaining oil and the remaining package of cabbage.

4. Reduce heat to medium-low; return all of the cabbage to skillet. Combine the remaining apple juice mixture and the brown sugar; stir into cabbage. Add fennel seed. Cook and stir for 2 to 3 minutes or until heated through.

5. Transfer cabbage mixture to a serving platter. Using a slotted spoon, remove fennel wedges from the liquid; discard liquid. Place fennel on top of cabbage mixture. Garnish with the reserved chopped fennel leaves and leaf sprigs. *Makes 8 servings.*

Brussels Sprouts with Bacon

Start to finish: 40 minutes

  1¼   pounds Brussels sprouts
      3   slices slab bacon or thick bacon, diced
  1½   teaspoons snipped fresh thyme or
          ½ teaspoon dried thyme, crushed
    ¼   teaspoon salt
    ¼   teaspoon pepper

1. Trim sprouts and discard any discolored outer leaves. Halve large sprouts. In a covered medium saucepan, cook sprouts in a small amount of boiling, salted water for 8 to 10 minutes or until tender. Drain; rinse under cold water. Pat dry with paper towels. Set aside.

2. In a large skillet, cook bacon over medium heat for 3 to 5 minutes or just until cooked through but not crisp. Drain off fat. Reduce heat to medium-low.

3. Add sprouts, thyme, salt, and pepper to bacon in skillet. Cook about 2 minutes or until sprouts are heated through. *Makes 8 servings.*

Three-Pea Medley

Three-Pea Medley
Start to finish: 20 minutes

⅓ cup water
1 medium carrot, sliced
3 cups fresh or frozen peas
2 cups fresh sugar snap peas
1 cup fresh snow pea pods
1 tablespoon olive oil
½ teaspoon finely shredded orange peel
¼ teaspoon salt
⅛ teaspoon pepper

1. In a 12-inch nonstick skillet, bring water to boiling. Add carrot; cover and cook over medium-high heat for 5 minutes.

2. Add fresh peas (if using); cook for 2 to 3 minutes. Add frozen peas (if using), sugar snap peas, snow pea pods, oil, orange peel, salt, and pepper.

3. Cook and stir for 3 to 5 minutes more or until vegetables are crisp-tender. *Makes 8 servings.*

The Pennsylvania Dutch often served a pea salad with turkey on Thanksgiving and Christmas. This contemporary spin adds pea pods.

21

Potatoes, whipped into a buttery mound and topped with meaty gravy, were a humble food that rich and poor alike could enjoy at holiday time. Throw in a few parsnips to make an American innovation, and don't forget the gravy!

Mashed Potatoes and Parsnips

Prep: 20 minutes • Cook: 20 minutes

1½ pounds russet potatoes (4 to 5 medium)
8 ounces parsnips
¼ cup butter or margarine, softened
¼ teaspoon salt
⅛ teaspoon pepper
¾ to 1 cup buttermilk, warmed slightly
¼ cup snipped Italian flat-leaf parsley

1. Peel and quarter the potatoes. Peel and cut the parsnips into large chunks. In a covered large saucepan, cook potatoes and parsnips in a small amount of boiling, lightly salted water for 20 to 25 minutes or until tender; drain.

2. Mash potatoes and parsnips with a potato masher or beat with an electric mixer on low speed. Add butter, salt, and pepper. Gradually beat in enough of the buttermilk to make a light and fluffy consistency. Spoon into a serving bowl. Sprinkle with parsley. *Makes 8 servings.*

Southern cooks think of sweet potatoes as their potato and often call them yams, although the two really are different vegetables. While you're more likely to eat mashed potatoes at a holiday dinner in the North, you can count on candied yams or sweet potatoes in the South almost anytime. Pictured on page 19.

Cider-Glazed Yams with Pears

Prep: 20 minutes • Cook: 10 minutes

2 pounds yams or sweet potatoes
3 tablespoons cornstarch
¼ teaspoon salt
¼ teaspoon ground allspice
2¼ cups apple juice or apple cider
½ cup golden raisins or chopped pitted dates
4 teaspoons lemon juice
4 ripe medium pears, cored and sliced

1. Peel yams. Cut off woody portions and ends; discard. Cut into 1-inch-thick pieces. In a covered large saucepan, cook yams in enough boiling water to cover about 10 minutes or until tender; drain.

2. Meanwhile, in another large saucepan, combine cornstarch, salt, and allspice. Stir in apple juice, raisins, and lemon juice. Cook and stir over medium heat until thickened and bubbly. Cook and stir for 2 minutes more. Gently stir in pears and yams; heat through. Serve warm. *Makes 8 servings.*

Make-Ahead Tip: Cook the yams and the sauce for Cider-Glazed Yams with Pears as directed; cover and refrigerate separately for up to 24 hours. To serve, stir the pears and cooked yams into the sauce; heat through. Be careful not to overcook because the yams may fall apart.

Candied Butternut Squash

Prep: 15 minutes • Bake: 1 hour

    2 medium butternut squash (about
          3 pounds total)
    ½ cup packed brown sugar
    3 tablespoons molasses
    3 tablespoons butter or margarine, softened
    1 teaspoon finely shredded orange peel
    ½ teaspoon ground cinnamon
    ¼ teaspoon ground cloves

1. Quarter squash lengthwise and remove seeds. Place quarters, cut sides down, in a 15×10×1-inch baking pan. Cover with foil; bake in a 350° oven for 40 minutes.

2. In a small bowl, combine brown sugar, molasses, butter, orange peel, cinnamon, and cloves.

3. Turn squash quarters so cut sides face up; drizzle with brown sugar mixture. Bake, uncovered, about 20 minutes more or until squash is tender. If desired, sprinkle with additional brown sugar and cloves. *Makes 8 servings.*

Wild Rice Pilaf

Prep: 20 minutes • Cook: 40 minutes

    ⅔ cup uncooked wild rice
    1 14-ounce can chicken broth
    1 cup water
    1 bay leaf
    1 teaspoon snipped fresh marjoram
          or ½ teaspoon dried marjoram, crushed
    ⅛ teaspoon pepper
    ⅔ cup uncooked long grain rice
    ½ cup coarsely chopped carrot
    ½ cup sliced celery
    ½ cup sliced leeks

1. Rinse wild rice in a strainer under cold running water about 1 minute.

2. In a medium saucepan, combine wild rice, chicken broth, the water, bay leaf, dried marjoram (if using), and pepper. Bring to boiling; reduce heat. Cover and simmer for 20 minutes.

3. Stir in long grain rice, carrot, celery, and leeks. Return to boiling; reduce heat. Cover and simmer about 20 minutes more or until rices are tender and liquid is absorbed. Stir in fresh marjoram, if using. Discard bay leaf. *Makes 6 servings.*

At the first Thanksgiving, the Indians introduced the Pilgrims to winter squash. The hardy vegetable has been a part of the American holiday table ever since. This recipe calls for butternut squash, but you can use other varieties such as acorn, banana, turban, Hubbard, or buttercup.

Wild rice takes a little longer to cook than regular rice, so it needs a head start. If you're serving this rice combo with the pork roast, start boiling the broth and water after you've covered the roast with foil. Pictured on page 18.

23

ndian pudding was originally a plain, stirred cornmeal mush. As time went on, colonial cooks added ingredients as they became available: molasses, butter, spices, milk, and eggs. Serve this comforting dessert with a little whipped cream and watch everyone scrape their bowls clean.

Sweet Indian Pudding

Prep: 15 minutes • Bake: 1 1/4 hours • Cool: 1 hour

      1 cup milk
    1/3 cup yellow cornmeal
      2 tablespoons butter, cut up
    1/3 cup molasses
    1/4 cup sugar
    1/2 teaspoon ground ginger
    1/2 teaspoon ground cinnamon
    1/4 teaspoon salt
      2 beaten eggs
  1 1/2 cups milk
        Whipped cream (optional)

1. In a medium saucepan, combine the 1 cup milk, the cornmeal, and butter. Bring to boiling, stirring constantly; reduce heat to low. Cover and cook for 5 minutes.

2. Remove saucepan from heat. Add molasses, sugar, ginger, cinnamon, and salt; stir until mixed.

3. In a small bowl, stir together eggs and the 1 1/2 cups milk; stir into cornmeal mixture. Turn mixture into an ungreased 1-quart casserole.

4. Bake, uncovered, in a 350° oven for 1 1/4 hours. Cool on a wire rack for 1 to 1 1/2 hours. Serve warm. If desired, top with whipped cream. *Makes 6 servings.*

Cranberry-Apricot Bread Pudding

Prep: 40 minutes • Bake: 45 minutes • Cool: 1 hour

     12 1/2-inch-thick slices French bread
      3 tablespoons snipped dried apricots
      3 tablespoons dried cranberries
      2 tablespoons butter, melted
  2 3/4 cups milk
    1/2 cup whipping cream
    1/2 of a vanilla bean, split lengthwise
      3 eggs
      3 egg yolks
    3/4 cup sugar
    1/8 teaspoon salt
      1 recipe Caramel Sauce

1. Trim crusts from bread; reserve for another use. Cut bread into 1-inch cubes; place in a single layer in a large shallow baking pan. Bake in a 300° oven 8 minutes or until slightly dry, turning once. Remove from oven; cool slightly. Meanwhile, butter a 1 1/2-quart soufflé dish or casserole; set aside.

2. Increase oven temperature to 350°. Place bread cubes, apricots, and cranberries in prepared dish. Drizzle with melted butter.

3. In a medium saucepan, heat milk, cream, and vanilla bean over medium heat until nearly boiling. Using a slotted spoon, remove vanilla bean; discard. Set aside.

4. Meanwhile, in a large bowl, beat together whole eggs and egg yolks with a rotary beater or wire whisk. Stir in sugar and salt. Gradually stir the hot milk mixture into the egg mixture. Pour evenly over bread cubes.

5. Place soufflé dish in a larger baking pan on the oven rack. Pour boiling water into larger pan around dish to a depth of 1 inch. Bake in the 350° oven for 45 to 50 minutes or until set around edge (center will be slightly moist but will continue to set on standing). Remove soufflé dish from hot water. Cool on a wire rack for 1 hour.

6. To serve, spoon bread pudding into dessert dishes. Serve with warm Caramel Sauce. *Makes 6 servings.*

Cranberry-Apricot Bread Pudding

"Waste not, want not" was the watchword of the pioneer cook. Every scrap of food was precious, and bread pudding was a good way to use leftover bread—as long as one had a chicken and a cow. As time went on, bread pudding reached lofty heights, as in the New Orleans' favorite with bourbon sauce. This cranberry-apricot rendition is also right up there.

Caramel Sauce: Combine 2 tablespoons *cold water* and 2 teaspoons *cornstarch*. Set aside. In a heavy, 10-inch skillet, place ½ cup *sugar*. Cook over medium-low heat without stirring until sugar begins to melt, shaking pan occasionally to heat the sugar evenly. Continue cooking, stirring occasionally with a wooden spoon, until a golden brown caramel syrup forms. Remove from heat. Carefully stir in ¾ cup *hot water*. (Sugar may resolidify.) Heat and stir over medium heat until sugar is dissolved. Stir cornstarch mixture; stir into syrup mixture in skillet. Bring to boiling. Cook and stir for 2 minutes more. Remove from heat. Add 1 tablespoon *butter* and 1 teaspoon *vanilla;* stir until smooth. Just before serving, reheat sauce if necessary.

25

Steamed Cranberry Pudding

Prep: 20 minutes • Steam: 1¾ hours • Cool: 15 minutes

In old England, plum pudding was called Christmas pudding and often was made on "Stir-Up Sunday" (the first Sunday of Advent) so it would be ready for the holiday. In this recipe, cranberries add a distinctly American twist to the English original.

2 cups fresh cranberries
2 tablespoons all-purpose flour
2 cups all-purpose flour
½ cup packed brown sugar
⅓ cup granulated sugar
1 teaspoon baking soda
1 teaspoon ground cinnamon
½ teaspoon ground nutmeg
¼ teaspoon ground allspice
1 cup milk
1 egg
2 tablespoons butter or margarine, melted
  Powdered sugar (optional)
  Sugared cranberries (optional)
  Fresh mint (optional)
1 recipe Vanilla Hard Sauce

1. In a medium bowl, stir together the 2 cups cranberries and the 2 tablespoons flour; set aside.

2. In a large bowl, stir together the 2 cups flour, brown sugar, granulated sugar, baking soda, cinnamon, nutmeg, and allspice. Add milk, egg, and melted butter; stir until mixed. Stir in cranberry mixture.

3. Transfer batter to a well-greased 7-cup metal mold. Lightly grease a square of foil; cover mold with foil, greased side down. Press foil tightly against rim of mold.

4. Place mold on a rack in a deep kettle containing 1 inch simmering water; cover kettle. Steam for 1¾ to 2 hours or until a wooden toothpick inserted near the center comes out clean, adding additional boiling water to kettle occasionally to maintain water level.

5. Remove pudding from kettle; remove foil. Cool in mold on a wire rack for 15 minutes. Carefully invert mold onto a wire rack; remove the mold. Cool slightly on rack.

6. Transfer pudding to a serving platter. If desired, sift powdered sugar over pudding and garnish with sugared cranberries and mint. Serve warm with Vanilla Hard Sauce. *Makes 12 servings.*

Vanilla Hard Sauce: In a small bowl, beat 1 cup sifted *powdered sugar* and ¼ cup softened *butter or margarine* with an electric mixer on medium speed for 3 to 5 minutes or until mixed. Beat in ½ teaspoon *vanilla*. Spoon into a serving bowl. Cover and refrigerate sauce to harden. *Makes ⅔ cup.*

Sugared Cranberries: Roll fresh *cranberries* in *sugar* until coated.

Steamed Cranberry Pudding

Pear and Mincemeat Tart

Prep: 45 minutes • Bake: 18 minutes • Chill: 2 hours

    2 medium red or yellow pears (such as
       Bartlett), peeled (if desired) and sliced
  ²⁄₃ cup orange juice
  ½ cup whipping cream
    1 8-ounce package cream cheese, softened
  ½ cup orange marmalade
    1 recipe Rich Tart Crust
 1¼ cups mincemeat
    1 cup desired fruit (such as halved seedless
       red or green grapes and/or
       mandarin orange sections)
  ¼ cup orange marmalade
       Pomegranate seeds (optional)

1. In a large skillet, combine pear slices and orange juice. Bring to boiling; reduce heat. Cover and simmer for 6 to 8 minutes or just until pears are tender. Drain pears, discarding liquid. Cover and refrigerate for at least 2 hours or up to 24 hours.

2. For filling, in a chilled small bowl, beat whipping cream with chilled beaters of an electric mixer on medium speed until soft peaks form; set aside. In a medium bowl, beat cream cheese and the ½ cup orange marmalade on medium speed until fluffy. Gently fold in whipped cream. Cover and refrigerate for up to 2 hours.

3. To assemble, spread mincemeat in baked tart shell. Spread with filling. Serve immediately or cover and refrigerate for up to 2 hours.

4. Before serving, remove side of tart pan and transfer tart to a serving platter. Arrange pear slices and desired fruit on top of the filling. In a small saucepan, heat the ¼ cup orange marmalade until melted; brush onto fruit. If desired, garnish with pomegranate seeds. *Makes 8 to 10 servings.*

Pear and Mincemeat Tart

Rich Tart Crust: In a medium bowl, stir together 1¼ cups *all-purpose flour* and ¼ cup *sugar.* Using a pastry blender, cut in ½ cup cold *butter* until pieces are pea-size. In a small bowl, stir together 2 beaten *egg yolks* and 2 tablespoons *water.* Gradually stir egg yolk mixture into flour mixture. Using your fingers, gently knead dough just until a ball forms. If necessary, cover with plastic wrap and refrigerate for 30 to 60 minutes or until dough is easy to handle.

On a lightly floured surface, slightly flatten dough. Roll from center to edge into a 13-inch circle. Wrap pastry around a rolling pin and unroll into an 11-inch tart pan with a removable bottom or a 10-inch pie plate or quiche dish. Ease pastry into pan, being careful not to stretch it. Press pastry into the fluted side of the pan; trim edge. Line pastry shell with a double thickness of foil.

Bake in a 350° oven for 10 minutes. Remove foil. Bake for 8 to 10 minutes more or until golden. Cool completely in pan on a wire rack.

Mincemeat pie has been traced back to the Crusaders who brought spices back to England from the Holy Land. The spices related to the Nativity and represented the gifts of the Magi. Superstition says refusing a slice of mincemeat pie brings bad luck. Although the mincemeat of colonial times contained meat, today's recipe is made from apples, raisins, spices, and candied fruit. Look for mincemeat near the pie fillings in your supermarket.

Sweet Potato Pie

Prep: 40 minutes • Bake: 48 minutes • Cool: 30 minutes • Chill: 2 hours

Sweet potatoes replace the Northern pumpkin in this Southern nut-topped pie. It's a modern-day adaptation of the sweet potato pies that have graced Southern holiday tables for hundreds of years.

1 pound sweet potatoes or one 17-ounce can sweet potatoes, drained
½ cup packed brown sugar
¼ cup butter, melted
1 tablespoon finely shredded orange peel
1 teaspoon ground cinnamon
½ teaspoon ground ginger
¼ teaspoon ground nutmeg
3 slightly beaten eggs
1 cup half-and-half or light cream
1 recipe Cornmeal Pastry
1 recipe Pecan Streusel Topping

1. If using fresh sweet potatoes, peel potatoes. Cut off woody portions and ends; discard. Cut sweet potatoes into quarters. In a covered large saucepan, cook sweet potatoes in enough boiling, salted water to cover for 25 to 35 minutes or until tender; drain.

2. In a medium bowl, mash drained fresh or canned sweet potatoes (you should have 1½ cups). Reserve any remaining sweet potatoes for another use. Stir in brown sugar, butter, orange peel, cinnamon, ginger, and nutmeg. Whisk in eggs and half-and-half.

3. Place Cornmeal Pastry shell on oven rack; pour in filling. Cover edge of pie with foil. Bake in a 375° oven for 30 minutes.

4. Remove foil. Sprinkle with Pecan Streusel Topping. Bake for 18 to 20 minutes more or until a knife inserted near center comes out clean. Cool on wire rack for 30 minutes. Chill at least 2 hours before serving; cover for longer storage. *Makes 8 servings.*

Cornmeal Pastry: In a medium bowl, stir together ¾ cup *all-purpose flour,* ½ cup *yellow cornmeal,* 1 tablespoon *sugar,* and ¼ teaspoon *salt.* Using a pastry blender, cut in ⅓ cup *shortening* until pieces are pea-size. Sprinkle 1 tablespoon *cold water* over part of the mixture; gently toss with a fork. Repeat moistening dough, using 1 tablespoon *cold water* at a time until all the dough is moistened (3 to 5 tablespoons *cold water* total). Form into a ball.

On a lightly floured surface, use your hands to slightly flatten dough. Roll dough from center to edge into a 12-inch circle. To transfer pastry, wrap it around the rolling pin. Unroll pastry into a 9-inch pie plate; ease pasty into pie plate, being careful not to stretch pastry. Trim to ½ inch beyond edge of plate. Fold under extra pastry; crimp edge high. Do not prick.

Pecan Streusel Topping: In a small bowl, stir together ¼ cup *all-purpose flour,* ¼ cup packed *brown sugar,* ⅛ teaspoon *ground cinnamon,* and ⅛ teaspoon *ground nutmeg.* Using a pastry blender, cut in 2 tablespoons *butter* until the mixture resembles coarse crumbs. Stir in ½ cup toasted, coarsely chopped *pecans.*

Sweet Potato Pie

Yule Log (Bûche de Noël)

Prep: 45 minutes • Bake: 12 minutes • Cool: 1 hour

    1   cup all-purpose flour
    ¼   teaspoon salt
    5   egg yolks
    2   tablespoons milk
    1   cup granulated sugar
    5   egg whites
    ¼   teaspoon cream of tartar
        Powdered sugar
    1   recipe Coffee-Cream Filling
    1   recipe Chocolate Buttercream Frosting

1. Grease and lightly flour a 15×10×1-inch jelly-roll pan; set aside.

2. In a small bowl, stir together flour and salt; set aside.

3. In a medium bowl, beat egg yolks and milk with an electric mixer on high speed about 5 minutes or until thick and lemon colored. Gradually add ½ cup of the granulated sugar, beating until sugar is almost dissolved.

4. Thoroughly wash beaters. In a very large bowl, beat egg whites and cream of tartar on medium to high speed until soft peaks form (tips curl). Gradually add the remaining granulated sugar, *2 tablespoons* at a time, beating on medium to high speed until stiff peaks form (tips stand straight).

5. Fold *1 cup* of the beaten egg whites into yolk mixture. Fold yolk mixture into remaining beaten egg whites. Fold in flour mixture just until combined. Spread batter evenly in prepared pan.

6. Bake in a 375° oven for 12 to 15 minutes or until cake springs back when lightly touched with a finger.

7. Immediately loosen edges of cake from pan. Turn cake out onto a towel sprinkled with powdered sugar. Roll up warm cake and towel, jelly-roll style, starting from a short side. Cool on a wire rack about 1 hour or until completely cooled.

8. Gently unroll cake. Spread Coffee-Cream Filling onto cake to within 1 inch of the edges. Roll up cake without towel. Cut a 1½-inch-thick slice from one end of cake.

9. Frost cake with Chocolate Buttercream Frosting. Place the slice on side of log to form a branch. Frost branch. Using the tines of a fork, score the cake lengthwise to resemble tree bark. Serve immediately or refrigerate up to 4 hours before serving. *Makes 10 servings.*

Coffee-Cream Filling: In a chilled small bowl, beat 1 cup *whipping cream,* ¼ cup sifted *powdered sugar,* and 1½ teaspoons *instant coffee crystals* with chilled beaters of an electric mixer on medium speed until soft peaks form (tips curl). *Makes about 2 cups.*

Chocolate Buttercream Frosting: In a medium bowl, beat ¼ cup *butter* with an electric mixer on medium to high speed until fluffy. Beat in ⅓ cup *unsweetened cocoa powder.* Gradually beat in 1½ cups sifted *powdered sugar.* Slowly beat in 3 tablespoons *milk* and 1 teaspoon *vanilla.* Slowly beat in 1½ cups sifted *powdered sugar.* If necessary, beat in enough *milk* to reach spreading consistency. *Makes about 1½ cups.*

Called Bûche de Noël *(log of Christmas) by the French Canadians, this cream-filled jelly-roll cake is made to resemble a log, a symbol of the warm fire burning in the Christmas hearth.*

Brandied Apple and Black Walnut Cake

Brandied Apple and Black Walnut Cake

Prep: 50 minutes • Bake: 35 minutes • Stand: 20 minutes

    2 cups all-purpose flour
    2 cups granulated sugar
    2 teaspoons baking powder
 1½ teaspoons ground cinnamon
    ½ teaspoon baking soda
    ¼ teaspoon salt
    ¼ teaspoon ground mace or ground nutmeg
    ¼ teaspoon ground cloves
    2 cups finely chopped peeled apples
    3 slightly beaten eggs
    ¾ cup chopped black walnuts or English
         walnuts, toasted
    ½ cup buttermilk
    ¼ cup cooking oil
    1 recipe Apple Glaze
    1 recipe Brandied Cream Cheese Frosting

1. Grease and lightly flour two 9×1½-inch round baking pans; set aside.

2. In a large bowl, stir together the flour, granulated sugar, baking powder, cinnamon, baking soda, salt, mace, and cloves. Stir in chopped apples, eggs, walnuts, buttermilk, and oil. Spread batter into prepared pans.

3. Bake in a 350° oven for 35 to 40 minutes or until a wooden toothpick inserted near centers comes out clean. Cool cakes in pans on wire racks for 15 minutes. Remove from pans; cool completely on wire racks.

4. Place a cake layer on a serving platter. Spoon hot Apple Glaze over top of layer. Let stand about 20 minutes or until set.

5. Meanwhile, prepare Brandied Cream Cheese Frosting. Spread about ¾ *cup* of the frosting over glazed cake layer. Top with the remaining cake layer. Frost cake top and side with frosting. Cover and store any remaining cake in the refrigerator. *Makes 16 servings.*

Apple Glaze: In a small saucepan, stir together 2 tablespoons *granulated sugar,* 2 tablespoons *brown sugar,* 2 tablespoons *butter,* 1 tablespoon *buttermilk,* and 1 teaspoon *light-colored corn syrup.* Bring to boiling; reduce heat. Cook and stir for 2 to 3 minutes or until reduced to ¼ cup. Remove from heat. Stir in 1 tablespoon *apple brandy, apple juice, or apple cider.*

Brandied Cream Cheese Frosting: In a large bowl, beat one 8-ounce package *cream cheese,* softened; ½ cup *butter,* softened; and 1 tablespoon *apple brandy, apple juice, or apple cider* with an electric mixer on medium to high speed until light and fluffy. Gradually add 2 cups sifted *powdered sugar,* beating well. Gradually beat in an additional 2 to 2½ cups sifted *powdered sugar* to make a frosting of spreading consistency.

Scarce and expensive in the old country, nuts have long been a special food for the holidays. Settlers discovered that black walnuts were a North American original in abundant supply. They incorporated the strong-flavored nuts into their Christmas recipes, often substituting them for harder-to-find English walnuts. You can use either in this delicious apple-spice cake.

Appetizer Sampler

The British have their high tea, the Russians their *zakuski,* the Spanish their tapas, and the Chinese their dim sum, but only in America does it all come together in one flavorful nibble fest. Perhaps it was the advent of the all-American cocktail that fashioned our taste for little bits of this and that. Or maybe it was our tradition of hosting holiday open houses where guests freely come and go, pausing for just a bite. Anyone who's ever tried a buffalo wing or a nacho knows that Americans have raised the art of snacking to new heights. As the following recipes show, our holiday tables grow ever more inventive with bite-size gems that blend regional and traditional ethnic foods into new American favorites.

Tropical Shrimp Cocktail
(recipe, page 40)

MENU
A Taste of Tex-Mex

Arriba! Spicy foods inspired by Mexico and our Southwest have arrived on our party tables with their bold flavors and festive colors. They're so easy to make, you can whip up a few yourself or ask friends to bring something along.

Beef and Olive Empanaditas (recipe, page 36)

Pear and Almond Quesadillas (recipe, page 36)

Cilantro-Jalapeño Cheese Logs (recipe, page 38)

Baked Santa Fe Dip (recipe at right) or Cumin Guacamole Dip (recipe opposite)

Vegetable platter of avocado, tomato, sweet peppers, chayote, zucchini, and jicama

Tortilla chips and salsa

Margaritas or limeade

Mexican beer with lime wedges

Baked Santa Fe Dip

Baked Santa Fe Dip
Prep: 20 minutes • Bake: 25 minutes

2 cups shredded cheddar cheese (8 ounces)
1 cup shredded Monterey Jack or mozzarella cheese (4 ounces)
1 8¾-ounce can whole kernel corn, drained
½ cup light mayonnaise dressing or salad dressing
1 4-ounce can diced green chili peppers, drained
2 teaspoons finely chopped canned chipotle peppers in adobo sauce
¼ teaspoon garlic powder
1 medium tomato, seeded and chopped
¼ cup sliced green onions
2 tablespoons snipped fresh cilantro
  Tortilla chips and/or vegetable dippers (such as sweet pepper wedges, zucchini slices, and jicama slices)

1. In a large bowl, stir together cheeses, corn, mayonnaise dressing, green chili peppers, chipotle peppers, and garlic powder. Spread mixture in a 9-inch quiche dish, shallow 1-quart casserole, or 9-inch pie plate.

2. Bake in a 350° oven about 25 minutes or until heated through.

3. In a small bowl, combine tomato, green onions, and cilantro. To serve, spoon tomato mixture onto cheese mixture. Serve with tortilla chips and/or vegetable dippers. *Makes 28 servings.*

Make-Ahead Tip: Prepare cheese mixture for Baked Santa Fe Dip as directed, except do not bake. Cover and refrigerate for up to 24 hours. Bake and serve as directed.

Corn Fritters with Cilantro Cream Sauce
Start to finish: 30 minutes

1¼ cups all-purpose flour
½ cup yellow cornmeal
2 teaspoons baking powder
1 teaspoon chili powder
½ teaspoon salt
1 cup frozen whole kernel corn, thawed and
    drained, or one 8¾-ounce can whole
    kernel corn, drained
1 cup milk
⅓ cup finely chopped green or red sweet
    pepper
¼ cup finely chopped red onion
1 beaten egg
  Cooking oil for deep-fat frying
1 recipe Cilantro Cream Sauce

1. In a medium bowl, stir together flour, cornmeal, baking powder, chili powder, and salt. Add corn, milk, sweet pepper, onion, and egg. Stir just until moistened.

2. Pour oil into a heavy, deep saucepan to a depth of 2½ to 3 inches. Heat oil to 375°. Drop batter by tablespoons, 4 or 5 at a time, into hot oil. Cook for 3 to 4 minutes or until golden brown, turning once. Drain fritters on paper towels. Keep fritters warm in a 300° oven while cooking the remaining fritters. Serve warm with Cilantro Cream Sauce. *Makes about 32 fritters.*

Cilantro Cream Sauce: In a medium bowl, stir together one 8-ounce carton *dairy sour cream,* ¼ cup finely chopped *red sweet pepper,* 1 tablespoon snipped *fresh cilantro,* 1 tablespoon *lime juice,* and ¼ teaspoon *chili powder.*

During the Civil War, resourceful cooks called corn fritters "mock oysters" because oysters from the North were unavailable for the holidays. They're also known as hush puppies in the South because cooks reportedly threw the fried batter to barking dogs to quiet them. This contemporary version takes a Southwest spin with some chili powder and a cilantro-lime dipping sauce.

Cumin Guacamole Dip
Start to finish: 15 minutes

2 teaspoons cumin seed
2 very ripe avocados, halved, seeded, peeled,
    and cut up
1 teaspoon finely shredded lime peel
1 tablespoon lime juice
¼ teaspoon salt
⅛ teaspoon ground red pepper
  Tortilla chips and/or vegetable dippers (such
    as baby carrots, cucumber slices, and
    broccoli florets)

1. In a small skillet, heat cumin seed over medium-high heat for 1 to 2 minutes or until lightly toasted, shaking skillet occasionally. Remove seed from skillet; cool. Coarsely crush cumin seed; set aside.

2. In a medium bowl, coarsely mash avocados with a fork. (If avocados are too firm to mash with a fork, use a food processor to coarsely mash them.)

3. Add lime peel, lime juice, salt, and red pepper. Stir in cumin seed. Serve with tortilla chips and/or vegetable dippers. *Makes about 1¼ cups.*

Make-Ahead Tip: Prepare Cumin Guacamole Dip as directed. Cover the surface with plastic wrap and refrigerate up to 24 hours (the color of the dip may darken upon chilling). Serve with tortilla chips and/or vegetable dippers.

Originally served by Montezuma to the Spaniards, "guacamole" means "poor man's butter," a testament to the abundance of avocados in Mexico. With its green color, guacamole is a favorite on our holiday party tables, especially when teamed with red salsa and tortilla chips.

Beef and Olive Empanaditas

Prep: 1 hour • Bake: 15 minutes

In Mexico and the southwestern United States, these little fried pies are a Christmas treat, often served between meals with red wine. Empanaditas can be either sweet or savory. This savory version has a picadillo filling (beef, raisins, and olives). Because it's baked rather than fried, it's easy to prepare for a holiday open house.

6 ounces lean ground beef
⅓ cup finely chopped onion
1 clove garlic, minced
½ teaspoon ground cumin
⅛ teaspoon ground red pepper
½ cup chopped pimiento-stuffed green olives
¼ cup tomato sauce
2 tablespoons golden raisins
1 recipe Empanadita Pastry
1 egg
1 tablespoon water

1. For filling, in a large skillet, cook beef, onion, and garlic until beef is brown. Drain off fat. Stir in cumin and red pepper. Cook and stir for 1 minute. Stir in olives, tomato sauce, and raisins. Set aside.

2. Place *1 rounded teaspoon* of the filling in the center of *each* dough round. Moisten edge with water; fold in half, sealing edge with tines of a fork. Prick dough several times. Place on ungreased baking sheet.

3. Stir together the egg and water; brush onto empanaditas. Bake in a 425° oven for 15 to 18 minutes or until golden. *Makes 36 empanaditas.*

Empanadita Pastry: For pastry, in a large bowl, stir together 3 cups *all-purpose flour* and ¼ teaspoon *salt*. Using a pastry blender, cut in ¾ cup *shortening* until mixture resembles cornmeal. Add ½ cup *milk* and 1 beaten *egg*; stir until mixed.

Turn dough out onto a lightly floured surface; knead for 10 to 12 strokes. Divide dough in half. Roll *one portion* of the dough to ⅛-inch thickness. Cut into 3-inch rounds; reroll scraps and cut enough additional rounds to make 18 total. Repeat with the remaining dough portion.

Make-Ahead Tip: Prepare Beef and Olive Empanaditas as directed, except do not bake. Cover and refrigerate up to 24 hours. Bake as directed.

Pear and Almond Quesadillas

Prep: 15 minutes • Cook: 6 minutes

The holiday tradition of the luminaria began in the Southwest, first with Indian bonfires, then with lanterns when the wagon trains began arriving in the 1820s. Today, candles glowing in paper bags illuminate sidewalks across the country at Christmas time. Set out some for your own Southwest holiday party.

2 medium ripe pears or apples, peeled and thinly sliced
1 tablespoon butter or margarine
1½ cups shredded Swiss or Monterey Jack cheese (6 ounces)
6 8-inch flour tortillas
⅓ cup sliced almonds, toasted
½ teaspoon caraway seed, crushed

1. In a medium skillet, cook pear slices in hot butter about 3 minutes or until crisp-tender, stirring occasionally. Remove from heat; drain pear slices on paper towels.

2. Sprinkle ¼ cup of the cheese over half of *each* tortilla. Divide pear slices, almonds, and caraway seed among tortillas. Fold tortillas in half, pressing gently.

3. Heat a large skillet over medium-high heat for 2 minutes; reduce heat to medium. Cook quesadillas, *two* at a time, in hot skillet for 2 to 3 minutes or until tortillas are light brown and cheese is melted, turning once. Remove from skillet. Keep warm in a 300° oven while cooking the remaining quesadillas. To serve, cut each quesadilla into 3 wedges. *Makes 18 servings.*

Beef and Olive Empanaditas

Cilantro-Jalapeño Cheese Logs

For an intriguing holiday snack, spread this spunky cheese mixture onto red tomato-flavored or green spinach-flavored flour tortillas. Then roll up the tortillas and cut them into slices to make festive spirals.

Cilantro-Jalapeño Cheese Logs
Prep: 25 minutes • Chill: 4 hours

2 cups shredded Monterey Jack cheese (8 ounces)
2 cups shredded sharp cheddar cheese (8 ounces)
1 8-ounce package cream cheese, softened
3 tablespoons finely chopped red sweet pepper
3 tablespoons snipped fresh cilantro
1 medium fresh jalapeño pepper, seeded and finely chopped
½ teaspoon Worcestershire sauce
2 tablespoons freshly ground whole pepper blend or seasoned pepper
Crackers and/or tortilla chips

1. In a large bowl, combine Monterey Jack, cheddar, and cream cheeses. Stir in sweet pepper, cilantro, jalapeño pepper, and Worcestershire sauce until combined.

2. Divide mixture in half. Shape each portion into a 5-inch-long log. Roll logs in freshly ground pepper. Wrap in plastic wrap or foil and refrigerate for at least 4 hours.

3. To serve, unwrap logs; cut into ¼-inch-thick slices and serve with crackers or tortilla chips. *Makes about 40 slices.*

Apricot-Glazed Riblets
Prep: 25 minutes • Bake: 1¼ hours

2½ to 3 pounds meaty pork loin back ribs
        or spareribs
 ½ cup orange marmalade
 ⅓ cup finely chopped onion
 ⅓ cup finely chopped dried apricots or figs
 3 tablespoons lemon juice
 2 tablespoons water
 1 teaspoon grated fresh ginger

1. Cut ribs into single-rib portions. Sprinkle ribs with *salt* and *pepper*. Arrange ribs, meaty sides up, in a shallow roasting pan. Bake in a 350° oven about 1 hour or until tender.

2. Meanwhile, for glaze, in a small saucepan, combine marmalade, onion, apricots, lemon juice, water, and ginger. Heat and stir until bubbly; reduce heat. Simmer, uncovered, about 5 minutes or until onion is tender. Set aside.

3. Drain fat from roasting pan. Brush ribs generously with glaze. Bake ribs for 15 minutes more, brushing with glaze during the last 5 minutes of baking. *Makes 14 to 18 servings.*

Cajun Party Mix
Prep: 10 minutes • Bake: 30 minutes

 4 cups popped popcorn
 2 cups pretzel sticks
 2 cups bite-size rice square cereal
 2 cups dry roasted peanuts
 ½ cup butter or margarine, melted
 1 tablespoon salt-free Cajun seasoning

1. In a large roasting pan, combine popcorn, pretzels, cereal, and peanuts; set aside.

2. In a small bowl, combine melted butter and Cajun seasoning; stir until mixed. Drizzle butter mixture over popcorn mixture; toss gently to coat.

3. Bake, uncovered, in a 300° oven for 30 minutes, stirring once. Spread on a piece of foil; cool. Store in an airtight container. *Makes about 9 cups.*

Spicy Pecans
Prep: 15 minutes • Bake: 15 minutes

 1 to 1½ teaspoons chili powder
 1 teaspoon garlic salt
 1 teaspoon curry powder
 ¼ teaspoon ground cumin
 ¼ teaspoon ground ginger
 ¼ teaspoon ground cinnamon
 3 tablespoons olive oil
 1 teaspoon Worcestershire sauce
 ¼ to ½ teaspoon bottled hot pepper sauce
 3 cups pecan halves

1. In a medium skillet, combine chili powder, garlic salt, curry powder, cumin, ginger, and cinnamon. Stir in olive oil, Worcestershire sauce, and hot pepper sauce. Cook and stir over low heat for 5 minutes.

2. Stir pecan halves into spice mixture, tossing to coat evenly. Spread pecan halves in a single layer in a 15×10×1-inch baking pan. Bake, uncovered, in a 325° oven about 15 minutes or until pecans are toasted, shaking pan occasionally. Cool completely. Store in an airtight container. *Makes 3 cups.*

S laves on Southern plantations fared better at Christmas time than at other times of the year. In Virginia, they might have made a favorite pork pie from pork back bones (spare ribs) discarded from the big house.

T he Acadians (Cajuns) were French-Canadians who settled in Louisiana during the late 1700s. They were poor people who preferred simple seasonings—peppers, celery, onion, thyme, and other herbs. This combination has become the background flavor of many modern-day holiday appetizers.

Tropical Shrimp Cocktail

Prep: 35 minutes • Marinate: 2 hours

1 tablespoon finely shredded lime or lemon peel
¼ cup lime or lemon juice
¼ cup olive oil or cooking oil
3 cloves garlic, minced
½ teaspoon coarse salt or salt
¼ teaspoon cracked black pepper
  Few drops bottled hot pepper sauce
1 pound peeled and deveined, cooked medium shrimp
  Kiwifruit, peeled and cut up, and mango or cantaloupe, peeled, seeded, and cut up
  Lime or lemon wedges (optional)

1. For marinade, in a small bowl, whisk together lime peel, lime juice, oil, garlic, salt, black pepper, and hot pepper sauce. Reserve *2 tablespoons* of the marinade; cover and refrigerate.

2. Rinse shrimp; pat dry. Place shrimp in a plastic bag set in a shallow dish. Pour the remaining marinade over shrimp in bag; seal bag. Marinate in the refrigerator for at least 2 hours or up to 4 hours, turning the bag occasionally.

3. To serve, drain shrimp, discarding marinade. Toss reserved marinade with fruit. Serve fruit with shrimp. If desired, serve with lime wedges. *Makes about 48 appetizers.*

Sesame Scallop Kabobs

Start to finish: 25 minutes

½ pound fresh or frozen bay scallops or small shrimp, peeled and deveined
  Nonstick cooking spray
1½ cups ¾-inch chunks fresh pineapple
½ cup bottled sweet ginger sesame sauce
1 cup sugar snap peas or snow pea pods, tips and strings removed

1. Thaw scallops, if frozen. Rinse scallops; pat dry. Line a 15×10×1-inch baking pan with foil; coat with nonstick cooking spray. Place scallops and pineapple in a single layer in prepared pan. Brush generously with ginger sesame sauce.

2. Broil about 4 inches from heat for 3 to 5 minutes or just until scallops are opaque and pineapple is heated through. Remove from broiler; cool for 5 minutes.

3. Meanwhile, in a small covered saucepan, cook snap peas in a small amount of boiling water for 1 minute; drain.

4. Thread pineapple and scallops onto party picks. Place a snap pea on the end of each pick. *Makes about 30 appetizers.*

Smoked Salmon-Cucumber Rounds

Start to finish: 20 minutes

  1 medium cucumber
  6 to 8 ounces thinly sliced smoked salmon
       (lox-style)
⅓ cup mayonnaise or salad dressing
  1 tablespoon snipped fresh dill
  1 teaspoon finely shredded lemon peel
  1 teaspoon lemon juice
      Fresh dill sprigs or finely shredded
       lemon peel

1. If desired, score cucumber by drawing the tip of a teaspoon or vegetable peeler lengthwise down cucumber at ½-inch intervals. Cut cucumber into ¼-inch-thick slices. Arrange slices on a serving platter.

2. Cut salmon into pieces to fit cucumber slices. Place a piece of salmon on top of each cucumber slice.

3. In a small bowl, combine mayonnaise, the snipped dill, lemon peel, and lemon juice. Spoon *½ teaspoon* of the mayonnaise mixture onto *each* piece of salmon. Garnish with dill sprigs. *Makes 20 to 24 rounds.*

Shrimp-Cucumber Rounds: Prepare Smoked Salmon-Cucumber Rounds as directed, except substitute ¾ pound peeled and deveined, cooked *medium shrimp* for the salmon. Spoon mayonnaise mixture onto each cucumber slice, then top each with a shrimp.

Make-Ahead Tip: Prepare Smoked Salmon-Cucumber Rounds or Shrimp-Cucumber Rounds as directed. Cover and refrigerate up to 1 hour before serving.

In Alaska and the Pacific Northwest, the Inuit people and American Indians have smoked salmon over cedar for centuries. Simple flavors bring out the taste of smoked salmon, such as the lemon and dill in these elegant canapés.

Smoked Salmon-Cucumber Rounds

Swedish Stuffed Potatoes

Prep: 25 minutes • Bake: 20 minutes

1½ pounds small new potatoes
   Olive oil or cooking oil
   Salt
   Pepper
¾ cup finely chopped, seeded cucumber
½ cup dairy sour cream
2 teaspoons snipped fresh dill or basil or
   ½ teaspoon dried dillweed or basil,
   crushed
   Snipped fresh dill or basil, caviar, sliced
   green onions, and/or chopped pimiento

1. Cut potatoes in half. Place potatoes, cut sides down, on a foil-lined baking sheet. Brush lightly with oil; sprinkle with salt and pepper. Bake in a 350° oven for 20 to 30 minutes or until tender. Let cool.

2. Place potato halves, cut sides up, on a flat surface. If necessary, cut a thin slice off the rounded side of each potato half so it sits upright.

3. In a small bowl, stir together cucumber, sour cream, and the 2 teaspoons dill. Spoon a small amount of the cucumber mixture on top of each potato. Garnish with fresh dill or basil, caviar, green onions, and/or pimiento. *Makes about 26 appetizers.*

Make-Ahead Tip: Prepare Swedish Stuffed Potatoes as directed. Cover and refrigerate up to 4 hours before serving.

Swedish Stuffed Potatoes

Creamy Dill Dip
Prep: 10 minutes • Chill: 1 hour

1 8-ounce package cream cheese, softened
1 8-ounce carton dairy sour cream
2 tablespoons finely chopped green onion
2 tablespoons snipped fresh dill or
    2 teaspoons dried dillweed
½ teaspoon seasoned salt or salt
   Milk (optional)
   Assorted vegetable dippers, crackers,
    and/or chips

In a medium bowl, beat cream cheese, sour cream, green onion, dill, and salt with an electric mixer on low speed until fluffy. Cover and refrigerate for at least 1 hour or up to 24 hours. If dip is too thick after chilling, stir in 1 to 2 tablespoons milk. Serve with vegetable dippers, crackers, and/or chips. *Makes about 2 cups.*

Creamy Parmesan Dip: Prepare Creamy Dill Dip as directed, except omit dill and salt. Stir ⅓ cup grated *Parmesan cheese* (2 ounces) and 2 teaspoons *dried Italian seasoning* into the beaten cream cheese mixture.

Dip into the flavors of the Midwest with colorful vegetable dippers—carrots, zucchini, broccoli, radishes, mushrooms, and pea pods. This creamy dip reflects the heartland's Scandinavian heritage and showcases its farm-fresh dairy products.

Blue Cheese Puffs
Prep: 45 minutes • Bake: 25 minutes

1 cup water
½ cup butter or margarine
⅛ teaspoon salt
1 cup all-purpose flour
4 eggs
1 cup crumbled blue cheese (4 ounces)
½ cup mayonnaise or salad dressing
1 tablespoon snipped fresh chives
30 spinach leaves (about 1 cup)
¾ pound deli-sliced roast beef or smoked
    turkey, cut into thin, bite-size strips

1. Grease 2 baking sheets; set aside. In a medium saucepan, combine water, butter, and salt. Cook and stir over medium heat until mixture is boiling. Add flour all at once, stirring vigorously. Cook and stir until mixture forms a ball that doesn't separate. Remove from heat. Cool for 10 minutes.

2. Add eggs, one at a time, beating with a wooden spoon after each addition until smooth. Stir in *¾ cup* of the blue cheese until combined.

3. Drop batter by rounded teaspoons about 2 inches apart onto prepared baking sheets. Bake in a 400° oven for 25 to 30 minutes or until golden. Transfer to a wire rack. Cool.

4. In a small bowl, stir together mayonnaise, chives, and remaining blue cheese.

5. To serve, cut tops from puffs. Place a spinach leaf in the bottom of each puff. Top *each* with some of the roast beef strips and about *1 teaspoon* of the mayonnaise mixture. Replace tops. *Makes about 30 appetizers.*

Some of the best blue cheese in the world is produced in our nation's heartland. It's often served at holiday time as part of a cheese tray or in appetizers, such as these mini blue cheese cream puffs. Serve them plain, with the blue cheese filling, or with the roast beef or turkey.

Spinach and Parmesan Phyllo Tarts

Prep: 25 minutes • Bake: 17 minutes

Many Greek immigrants settled in such cities as Chicago and New York, often opening restaurants or shops to share their phyllo treats and other specialities. For this easy Greek-style holiday appetizer, you'll need to thaw the phyllo dough and spinach soufflé ahead of time. You can refreeze any unused phyllo dough if you wrap it tightly.

Nonstick cooking spray
4 sheets frozen phyllo dough
   (18×14-inch rectangles), thawed
3 to 4 tablespoons butter or margarine,
   melted
1 12-ounce package frozen spinach soufflé,
   thawed
¼ cup finely shredded Parmesan cheese

1. Lightly coat twenty-four 1¾-inch muffin cups with nonstick cooking spray; set aside. To make phyllo cups, unroll dough sheets. Carefully transfer the top sheet to a large cutting board. Brush with some of the melted butter. Place a second sheet on top of the first sheet; brush again with butter. Repeat with remaining phyllo sheets and melted butter to make one stack, brushing all edges of dough to keep moist.

2. Cut phyllo stack lengthwise into quarters. Cut each quarter into 6 squares, making 24 squares total. Place one square in *each* prepared muffin cup, pleating phyllo as necessary to form a cup. (If not enough muffin cups are available, cover remaining dough squares with plastic wrap and a damp towel until needed.) Spoon a *scant tablespoon* of the thawed spinach soufflé into *each* phyllo cup.

3. Bake in a 350° oven about 15 minutes or until a knife inserted near centers comes out clean. Sprinkle with Parmesan cheese. Bake for 2 to 3 minutes more or until cheese is melted. Serve warm. *Makes 24 servings.*

Spinach and Parmesan Phyllo Tarts

Feta and Pine Nut Roll-Ups
Prep: 25 minutes • Bake: 18 minutes

1 3-ounce package cream cheese, softened
½ cup crumbled feta cheese with garlic and
    herbs
3 tablespoons pine nuts or finely chopped
    almonds, toasted
3 tablespoons finely chopped pitted ripe olives
2 tablespoons snipped fresh parsley
1 tablespoon milk
1 10-ounce package refrigerated pizza dough
    Olive oil
    Pepper

1. For filling, in a small bowl, stir together cream cheese, feta cheese, nuts, olives, parsley, and milk until combined. Set aside.

2. Grease a baking sheet; set aside. On a lightly floured surface, roll pizza dough into a 14×10-inch rectangle. Cut dough in half crosswise to form two 10×7-inch rectangles. Spread *half* of the filling onto *each* dough rectangle to within 1 inch of edges. Starting from a long side, roll up each rectangle into a spiral. Seal seam and ends. Place rolls, seam sides down, on prepared baking sheet. Brush surface of rolls with oil; sprinkle with pepper.

3. Bake in a 350° oven for 18 to 20 minutes or until golden. Cool on baking sheet on a wire rack for 5 minutes. Using a serrated knife, cut rolls crosswise into 1-inch-thick slices. Serve warm. *Makes 20 servings.*

I f you'd rather serve this Greek-style filling as a dip, combine the cheeses with the nuts, olives, and parsley, then stir in enough milk to make it a dipping consistency. Serve the dip with toasted pita bread wedges.

Buffalo Chicken Wings
Prep: 20 minutes • Grill: 18 minutes

16 chicken wings (about 3 pounds total)
2 tablespoons butter or margarine
1 2-ounce bottle hot pepper sauce (¼ cup)
1 recipe Blue Cheese Dip
    Celery sticks

1. For a charcoal grill, preheat coals; test for medium heat. For a gas grill, preheat grill; reduce heat to medium.

2. Cut off and discard wing tips. Bend the two larger sections of each wing back and forth, breaking the cartilage connecting them. Using a knife or cleaver, cut through the cartilage and skin, cutting each wing into 2 sections.

3. In a small saucepan, melt butter. Stir in hot pepper sauce. Brush some of the mixture onto chicken pieces.

4. Arrange chicken pieces on the rack over the coals. Grill, uncovered, directly over heat for 18 to 20 minutes or until tender and no longer pink, turning once and brushing with remaining butter mixture halfway through grilling.

5. Serve chicken pieces with Blue Cheese Dip and celery sticks. *Makes 32 servings.*

Blue Cheese Dip: In a blender container or food processor bowl, combine ½ cup *dairy sour cream,* ½ cup crumbled *blue cheese,* ¼ cup *mayonnaise or salad dressing,* 2 tablespoons thinly sliced *green onion,* 2 tablespoons *lemon juice,* 1 tablespoon *milk,* and 2 cloves *garlic,* minced. Cover and blend or process just until combined. Transfer the dip to a small bowl; cover and refrigerate for 1 hour. *Makes about 1¼ cups.*

T he Anchor Bar in Buffalo, New York, takes credit for inventing these blazing chicken wings tempered by a creamy blue cheese dip. They're a mainstay now on many holiday cocktail buffets. For a festive accent, serve the blue cheese dip in bowls made from green and red sweet pepper halves.

Artichoke and Olive Pizza Wedges

Prep: 25 minutes • Bake: 8 minutes

  1 12-inch Italian bread shell (Boboli)
  1 6-ounce jar marinated artichoke hearts, drained
1¼ cups shredded mozzarella cheese (5 ounces)
  1 cup sliced fresh mushrooms
⅓ cup pitted Greek black olives or ripe olives, drained and sliced
  2 tablespoons sliced pimiento, drained
  1 to 2 tablespoons snipped fresh basil
  2 teaspoons snipped fresh thyme
⅓ cup finely shredded Parmesan cheese

1. Place bread shell on a baking sheet or pizza pan; set aside. If necessary, cut up any large artichoke heart pieces.

2. Sprinkle *1 cup* of the mozzarella cheese over bread shell. Top with artichoke pieces, mushrooms, olives, pimiento, basil, and thyme. Sprinkle with remaining mozzarella cheese and the Parmesan cheese.

3. Bake in a 450° oven for 8 to 10 minutes or until cheese is melted. Cut into wedges and serve warm. *Makes 16 servings.*

Pepper Jack and Pistachio Bruschetta

Start to finish: 30 minutes

⅓ cup olive oil or cooking oil
  1 tablespoon snipped fresh oregano or basil
  1 loaf baguette-style French bread
  4 roma tomatoes, thinly sliced
  8 ounces Monterey Jack cheese with jalapeño peppers, thinly sliced
¼ cup chopped pistachio nuts or pine nuts

1. In a small bowl, combine oil and oregano; set aside. Slice bread diagonally into ½-inch-thick slices. (You should have about 24 slices.) Brush both sides of slices lightly with oil mixture.

2. Place slices on a large baking sheet. Broil 4 to 6 inches from the heat for 1 to 1½ minutes or just until light brown.

3. Turn slices over. Place *one* tomato slice on *each* bread slice. Cut cheese slices to fit bread. Place *one* cheese slice on *each* tomato slice; sprinkle with pistachio nuts. Broil for 2 to 2½ minutes more or just until cheese is melted. Serve warm. *Makes about 24 servings.*

Pasta Party Mix

T ri-colored rotini pasta dresses up this crispy snack mix. When you want a change of pace, omit the herbs and other seasonings and toss the fried pasta with about 2 tablespoons of taco seasoning mix.

Pasta Party Mix
Prep: 20 minutes • Stand: 15 minutes • Cook: 24 minutes

    8 ounces dried tri-colored rotini pasta
        (about 3 cups)
    4 ounces dried penne pasta (about 1½ cups)
    4 ounces dried bow-tie pasta
        (about 1¾ cups)
 1½ teaspoons seasoned salt
    1 teaspoon dried basil, crushed
    1 teaspoon dried oregano, crushed
    1 teaspoon dried thyme, crushed
   ½ teaspoon paprika
   ¼ teaspoon garlic powder
        Cooking oil for deep fat-frying

1. In a Dutch oven, cook pastas together in a large amount of boiling salted water about 11 minutes or just until tender. Drain in a colander; rinse with cold water. Let stand in colander about 15 minutes to thoroughly drain. Pat dry with paper towels.

2. Meanwhile, in a small bowl, stir together seasoned salt, basil, oregano, thyme, paprika, and garlic powder; set aside.

3. In a heavy, deep saucepan or wok, heat 3 inches of oil to 365°. Fry cooked pasta, about ⅓ *cup* at a time, in hot oil for 1 to 2 minutes or until golden and crisp (be sure pasta is very dry; oil will foam when pasta is added). Using a slotted spoon, remove pasta and drain on paper towels.

4. Sprinkle pasta with herb mixture. (Or place herb mixture in a large plastic bag. Add 2 to 3 cups pasta; seal bag and shake to coat. Repeat to coat remaining pasta.) *Makes about 12 cups.*

Apple Cinnamon Rolls (recipe, page 56)

Heartwarming Breakfasts

William Byrd II of Westover, Virginia, noted in his journal on Christmas Day, 1709, that he feasted on broiled turkey for breakfast. Our holiday breakfast has come a long way since then. Many American families today start their holiday morning with stacks of fluffy hotcakes glistening in maple syrup or crispy waffles heaped with berries. Others dish up egg casseroles oozing with cheese or giant cinnamon rolls crowned with glaze. To satisfy all your morning cravings this time of year, we've created several menus. For a taste of our most heartwarming breakfast and brunch foods, turn the page.

Here's a breakfast you can put together before any of your creatures are stirring, then take a shower while it bakes.

Sliced kiwi fruit and strawberries

Baked Orange French Toast with Marmalade Sauce (recipe at right)

Breakfast sausage

Orange or grapefruit juice

Coffee or tea

Baked Orange French Toast
Prep: 20 minutes • Bake: 35 minutes

¼ cup sugar
1 teaspoon ground cinnamon
6 eggs
1¾ cups milk
⅓ cup orange marmalade
½ teaspoon vanilla
6 slices dry whole wheat bread,* cut into
    1-inch cubes
⅓ cup raisins
1 recipe Marmalade Sauce

1. In a medium bowl, combine sugar and cinnamon. Add eggs, milk, orange marmalade, and vanilla; whisk to combine.

2. In a large bowl, combine bread cubes and raisins; arrange in an ungreased 2-quart rectangular baking pan. Pour egg mixture over all.

3. Bake in a 325° oven for 35 minutes (center may appear slightly wet but will set during standing). Cool on a wire rack for 10 minutes. Serve warm topped with Marmalade Sauce. *Makes 6 servings.*

Marmalade Sauce: In a small saucepan, combine 1 tablespoon *cornstarch* and ½ teaspoon finely shredded *orange peel*. Stir in ¾ cup *orange juice* and ⅓ cup *orange marmalade*. Cook and stir over medium-low heat until thickened and bubbly. Remove from heat; if desired, stir in 2 teaspoons *butter*. Serve warm. *Makes 1 cup.*

*****Note:** To dry bread, place slices on a wire rack and let stand at least 4 hours.

Blueberry Syrup
Prep: 5 minutes • Cook: 25 minutes

2 cups fresh or frozen blueberries
½ cup water
¼ cup sugar
2 teaspoons lime juice or lemon juice

1. In a medium saucepan, combine *1 cup* of the blueberries, the water, sugar, and lime juice. Cook and stir over medium heat for 2 to 3 minutes or until sugar is dissolved. Bring mixture to boiling; reduce heat. Simmer, uncovered, for 15 to 20 minutes or until slightly thickened, stirring occasionally.

2. Stir in remaining blueberries. Cook, stirring occasionally, for 2 to 3 minutes more or until blueberries are soft. Cool slightly.

3. Pour blueberry mixture into a blender container. Cover and blend until smooth. Serve warm or cover and refrigerate for up to 1 week. *Makes about 1 cup.*

Eggs Benedict

Start to finish: 35 minutes

4 eggs
2 English muffins, split
4 slices Canadian-style bacon
1 recipe Hollandaise Sauce
    Paprika

1. Lightly grease a medium skillet. Add water to half-fill the skillet. Bring water to boiling; reduce heat to simmering (bubbles should begin to break the surface of the water).

2. Break *one* of the eggs into a measuring cup. Carefully slide egg into simmering water, holding the lip of the cup as close to the water as possible. Repeat with remaining eggs, allowing each egg an equal amount of space. Simmer eggs, uncovered, for 3 to 5 minutes or until the whites are completely set and yolks begin to thicken but are not hard. Using a slotted spoon, remove poached eggs and place them in a large pan of warm water to keep warm.

3. Meanwhile, place muffin halves, cut sides up, on a baking sheet. Broil 3 to 4 inches

from heat about 2 minutes or until toasted.
4. Top *each* muffin half with *one slice* of Canadian-style bacon; broil about 1 minute more or until meat is heated through.

5. To serve, top *each* bacon-topped muffin half with *one egg;* spoon Hollandaise Sauce over eggs. Sprinkle with paprika. *Makes 4 servings.*

Hollandaise Sauce: Cut ½ cup *butter* into thirds and bring to room temperature. In the top of a double boiler, combine 3 beaten *egg yolks,* 1 tablespoon *lemon juice,* and 1 tablespoon *water.* Add a piece of the butter. Place over gently boiling water (upper pan should not touch water). Cook, stirring rapidly with a whisk, until butter melts and sauce begins to thicken. (Sauce may appear to curdle at this point, but will smooth out when remaining butter is added.) Add the remaining butter, a piece at a time, stirring constantly until melted. Continue to cook and stir for 2 to 2½ minutes more or until sauce thickens. Immediately remove from heat. If sauce is too thick or curdles, immediately whisk in 1 to 2 tablespoons *hot water.* Season to taste with *salt* and *pepper. Makes ¾ cup.*

Spiced Cider Syrup

Prep: 5 minutes • Cook: 30 minutes

¼ cup packed brown sugar
½ teaspoon ground cinnamon
¼ teaspoon ground nutmeg
⅛ teaspoon ground cloves
1½ cups apple cider or apple juice
1 tablespoon lemon juice
¼ cup apple jelly

1. In a medium saucepan, stir together brown sugar, cinnamon, nutmeg, and cloves. Stir in apple cider and lemon juice. Cook and stir over medium heat for 2 to 3 minutes or until sugar is dissolved. Stir in apple jelly.

2. Bring to boiling; reduce heat. Simmer, uncovered, about 30 minutes or until desired consistency, stirring occasionally. Serve warm or cover and refrigerate for up to 1 week. *Makes about ¾ cup.*

MENU

French Quarter Brunch for 4

Since the early 1900s, a holiday brunch at Brennan's restaurant in New Orleans has called for Eggs Benedict, followed by a stroll to Café du Monde for beignets and café au lait.

Mimosas

Eggs Benedict (recipe at left)

Steamed asparagus spears or tomato slices

Cheesy Corn and Grits (recipe, page 58)

*Nutmeg Beignets (recipe, page 55)
or
Lemon Burst Biscuits (recipe, page 57)*

Café au lait

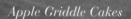
Apple Griddle Cakes

Apple Griddle Cakes
Prep: 25 minutes • Cook: 16 minutes

C all 'em griddle cakes, hotcakes, flapjacks, sweat pads, or pancakes, these fluffy, filling disks were a favorite of lumberjacks and still make a hearty meal on wintery holiday mornings. Modeled after the thin Swedish pancake and French crepe, there's nothing dainty about this American cousin. Keep yourn stack warm in a loosely covered ovenproof dish in a 300° oven.

- 2 large cooking apples (such as Jonathan or Granny Smith), peeled (if desired) and finely chopped (about 1½ cups)
- 2 teaspoons lemon juice
- 1½ cups whole wheat flour
- 2 tablespoons sugar
- 2 teaspoons baking powder
- ½ teaspoon ground cinnamon
- ¼ teaspoon salt
- 1 slightly beaten egg
- 1½ cups milk
- 3 tablespoons cooking oil or melted butter
- 1 recipe Spiced Cider Syrup, pure maple syrup, or maple-flavored syrup

1. In a medium bowl, combine apples and lemon juice. In another medium bowl, combine flour, sugar, baking powder, cinnamon, and salt. In a small bowl, combine egg, milk, and oil. Set aside.

2. Add egg mixture all at once to flour mixture; stir just until moistened (the batter should be lumpy). Gently fold in the apple mixture.

3. Heat a lightly greased griddle or heavy skillet over medium heat until a few drops of water dance across the surface. For *each* pancake, pour a scant ¼ *cup* of the batter onto the hot griddle; spread batter into 4-inch circle.

4. Cook for 1 to 2 minutes on each side or until pancakes are golden, turning to second sides when pancake surfaces are bubbly and edges are slightly dry, adding oil to griddle as necessary. Serve warm with syrup. *Makes 16 (4-inch) pancakes.*

Pumpkin Waffles
Prep: 15 minutes • Cook: per waffle baker directions

2 cups whole wheat flour
2 tablespoons brown sugar
1 tablespoon baking powder
1 teaspoon ground cinnamon
½ teaspoon salt
¼ teaspoon baking soda
¼ teaspoon ground nutmeg
¼ teaspoon ground ginger
1¾ cups milk
1 cup canned pumpkin or mashed, cooked
   pumpkin
2 egg yolks
3 tablespoons butter, melted
1 teaspoon finely shredded orange peel
   (optional)
2 egg whites
1 recipe Cider-Honey Syrup (optional)

1. In a large bowl, stir together flour, brown sugar, baking powder, cinnamon, salt, baking soda, nutmeg, and ginger; set aside.

2. In a medium bowl, combine milk, pumpkin, egg yolks, butter, and, if desired, orange peel. Add pumpkin mixture all at once to flour mixture; stir just until combined (batter should be lumpy).

3. In a small bowl, beat egg whites with an electric mixer on high speed until stiff peaks form (tips stand straight). Gently fold beaten egg whites into pumpkin mixture, leaving a few puffs of egg white.

4. Heat a lightly greased waffle baker. Pour some of the batter onto the waffle grids. Close lid quickly; do not open until done. Bake according to manufacturer's directions. When done, use a fork to lift waffle off grids. Repeat with remaining batter.

5. Serve waffles immediately or keep warm in a loosely covered ovenproof dish in a 300° oven. If desired, serve with Cider-Honey Syrup. *Makes 16 (4-inch) waffles.*

Cider-Honey Syrup: In a small saucepan, combine 1 cup *apple cider or apple juice* and 1 cup *honey.* Bring to boiling; reduce heat. Simmer, uncovered, for 15 to 20 minutes or until slightly thickened. Serve warm. Cover and store any remaining syrup in the refrigerator for up to 1 week. *Makes about 1 cup.*

MENU

Pancake Breakfast for 4 to 6

Community pancake breakfasts have become an American tradition. Put on your own pancake (or waffle) breakfast over the holidays and watch the kids stack 'em high.

Melon, berries, and orange wedges

Apple Griddle Cakes (recipe opposite) with Spiced Cider Syrup (recipe, page 51) or Pumpkin Waffles with Cider-Honey Syrup (recipe at left)

Bacon or ham

Cranberry or apple juice

Coffee or tea

Pumpkin Waffles

Maple Bran Muffins

Maple Bran Muffins

Prep: 25 minutes • Bake: 30 minutes

1⅔ cups buttermilk
2⅔ cups whole bran cereal
  1 cup whole wheat flour
1¾ teaspoons baking powder
  ¼ teaspoon baking soda
  3 tablespoons cooking oil
  2 tablespoons butter, softened
  ⅓ cup packed brown sugar
  2 eggs
  ¼ cup pure maple syrup or maple-flavored syrup
  ¾ cup raisins or mixed dried fruit bits

1. Lightly grease six 3¼-inch muffin cups or twelve 2½-inch muffin cups; set aside. In a medium bowl, pour buttermilk over the bran cereal; let stand for 5 to 10 minutes or until cereal is softened. In a small bowl, stir together flour, baking powder, and baking soda; set aside.

2. In a large bowl, beat oil and butter with an electric mixer on medium speed for 30 seconds. Add brown sugar; beat about 30 seconds or until fluffy. Beat in eggs, one at a time, until mixed. Add maple syrup; beat until combined.

3. Add cereal mixture and flour mixture to syrup mixture, stirring just until combined. Stir in raisins. Spoon batter into prepared muffin cups, filling each cup about ¾ full.

4. Bake in a 350° oven about 30 minutes or until tops are golden and centers are firm to the touch. Cool in muffin cups on a wire rack for 5 minutes. Remove from muffin cups. Serve warm. *Makes 6 large muffins or 12 regular muffins.*

Nutmeg Beignets

Prep: 40 minutes • Chill: 4 hours • Stand: 30 minutes total • Cook: 10 minutes

3 to 3¼ cups all-purpose flour
1 package active dry yeast
1¼ teaspoons grated whole nutmeg
    or 1 teaspoon ground nutmeg
1 cup milk
¼ cup granulated sugar
2 tablespoons shortening
½ teaspoon salt
1 egg
    Shortening or cooking oil for deep-fat frying
    Sifted powdered sugar (optional)

1. In a large bowl, stir together *1½ cups* of the flour, the yeast, and nutmeg. In a small saucepan, heat and stir milk, granulated sugar, the 2 tablespoons shortening, and the salt just until warm (120° to 130°) and shortening is almost melted.

2. Add milk mixture to flour mixture; add egg. Beat with an electric mixer on low to medium speed for 30 seconds, scraping side of bowl constantly. Beat on high speed for 3 minutes. Using a wooden spoon, stir in enough of the remaining flour to make a soft dough.

3. Place dough in a greased bowl; turn once to grease surface. Cover; refrigerate for at least 4 hours or up to 24 hours.

4. Punch down dough. Turn dough out onto a lightly floured surface. Cover; let rest for 10 minutes. Roll into a 15×12-inch rectangle; cut into thirty 3×2-inch rectangles. Cover; let rest for 20 minutes (dough will not double in size).

5. In a heavy, deep saucepan, heat 3 inches of shortening to 375°. Fry dough rectangles, a few at a time, in deep hot fat about 1 minute or until beignets are golden, turning once. Using a slotted spoon, remove beignets and drain on paper towels. Keep warm in a 300° oven while frying remaining beignets. If desired, sprinkle with powdered sugar. *Makes 30 beignets.*

A hallmark of New Orleans' French Quarter coffee houses, beignets (ben yayz) are square, hole-less doughnuts that are so airy and delicate, it's easy to wolf down two or three at a sitting. Be sure to use a deep saucepan for frying the beignets, leaving at least 3 inches between the oil and the top of the pan.

Caramel-Pecan Bubble Ring

Prep: 20 minutes • Bake: 35 minutes

⅓ cup chopped pecans
¾ cup sugar
4 teaspoons ground cinnamon
2 11-ounce packages refrigerated
    breadsticks (16 to 24 total)
⅓ cup butter or margarine, melted
½ cup caramel ice cream topping
2 tablespoons pure maple syrup or
    maple-flavored syrup

1. Generously grease a 10-inch fluted tube pan. Sprinkle *half* of the pecans in pan. Stir together sugar and cinnamon. Set aside.

2. Separate *each* package of breadsticks into *8 to 12* spirals. Do not unroll. Cut each spiral in half crosswise. Dip each piece of dough into melted butter, then into sugar mixture to coat.

3. Arrange dough pieces, spiral sides down, in the prepared pan, making two layers. Sprinkle dough with the remaining pecans. In a measuring cup, stir together caramel topping and maple syrup; drizzle over dough pieces.

4. Bake in a 350° oven about 35 minutes or until dough is light brown, covering with foil for the last 10 minutes of baking to prevent overbrowning, if necessary.

5. Let stand for 1 minute only. (If the ring stands for more than 1 minute, it will be difficult to remove from pan.) Invert onto a serving platter. Spoon any topping and nuts remaining in the pan onto ring. Serve warm. *Makes 12 servings.*

A gooey, sticky caramel-pecan roll is the South's answer to the cinnamon roll. This pull-apart bubble ring preserves the roll's traditional flavor, yet takes advantage of two convenient products: refrigerated breadstick dough and caramel ice cream topping.

Apple Cinnamon Rolls

Prep: 45 minutes • Rise: 1½ hours • Bake: 20 minutes

4¾ to 5¼ cups all-purpose four
1 package active dry yeast
1 cup milk
⅓ cup sugar
⅓ cup butter
½ teaspoon salt
3 eggs
1 recipe Cinnamon Filling
1 cup finely chopped, peeled apple
1 tablespoon half-and-half or light cream
1 recipe Vanilla Glaze

1. In a large bowl, stir together *2¼ cups* of the flour and the yeast. In a small saucepan, heat and stir milk, sugar, butter, and salt just until warm (120° to 130°) and butter is almost melted.

2. Add milk mixture to flour mixture; add eggs. Beat with an electric mixer on low to medium speed for 30 seconds, scraping side of bowl constantly. Beat on high speed for 3 minutes. Using a wooden spoon, stir in as much of the remaining flour as you can.

3. Turn dough out onto a lightly floured surface. Knead in enough of the remaining flour to make a moderately soft dough that is smooth and elastic (3 to 5 minutes total). Shape into a ball. Place in a lightly greased bowl; turn once to grease surface. Cover and let rise in a warm place until double in size (about 1 hour).

4. Punch dough down. Turn out onto a lightly floured surface. Divide in half. Cover and let rest for 10 minutes.

5. Roll *each* dough portion into a 12×8-inch rectangle. Sprinkle with Cinnamon Filling. Sprinkle with apple. Starting from a long side, roll up *each* rectangle into a spiral; seal seams. Slice *each* roll into 12 pieces.

6. Lightly grease two 9×1½-inch round baking pans or 2 baking sheets. Place rolls, cut sides down, in pans or on baking sheets.

7. Cover; let rise in warm place until nearly double in size (about 30 minutes).

8. Brush dough with *1 teaspoon* of the half-and-half. Bake in a 375° oven for 20 to 25 minutes or until light brown. If necessary to prevent overbrowning, cover rolls loosely with foil the last 5 to 10 minutes of baking.

9. Remove rolls from oven. Brush with the remaining half-and-half. Cool in pans for 1 minute. Carefully invert rolls onto wire racks. Cool slightly. Invert onto a serving platter. Drizzle with Vanilla Glaze. Serve warm. *Makes 24 rolls.*

Cinnamon Filling: In a medium bowl, stir together ¾ cup packed *brown sugar*, ¼ cup *all-purpose flour*, and 1 tablespoon *ground cinnamon*. Using a pastry blender, cut in ⅓ cup *butter* until crumbly.

Vanilla Glaze: In a small bowl, stir together 1¼ cups sifted *powdered sugar*, 1 teaspoon *light-colored corn syrup*, and ½ teaspoon *vanilla*. Stir in enough *half-and-half or light cream* (1 to 2 tablespoons) to make a glaze of drizzling consistency.

Chocolate Cinnamon Rolls: Prepare Apple Cinnamon Rolls as directed, except substitute 1 cup *semisweet chocolate pieces* for the chopped apple.

Raisin-Pecan Cinnamon Rolls: Prepare Apple Cinnamon Rolls as directed, except substitute ½ cup *golden raisins* and ½ cup chopped *pecans* for the chopped apple.

Make-Ahead Tip: Prepare Apple Cinnamon Rolls as directed, except cover pans of *unbaked* rolls loosely with plastic wrap, leaving room for rolls to rise. Refrigerate for at least 2 hours or up to 24 hours. Uncover; let stand at room temperature for 30 minutes. Break any surface bubbles with a greased toothpick. Brush with half-and-half and bake as directed.

Lemon Burst Biscuits

Lemon Burst Biscuits
Prep: 25 minutes • Bake: 10 minutes

  2 cups all-purpose flour
  1 tablespoon sugar
  2 teaspoons baking powder
  2 teaspoons finely shredded lemon peel
 $\frac{1}{4}$ teaspoon baking soda
 $\frac{1}{4}$ teaspoon salt
 $\frac{1}{3}$ cup shortening
 $\frac{1}{3}$ cup buttermilk
 $\frac{1}{3}$ cup mayonnaise or salad dressing
  1 recipe Lemon Glaze (optional)

1. In a large bowl, stir together flour, sugar, baking powder, lemon peel, baking soda, and salt. Using a pastry blender, cut in shortening until mixture resembles coarse crumbs. Make a well in the center of the flour mixture.

2. In a small bowl, combine buttermilk and mayonnaise; add to flour mixture all at once. Using a fork, stir just until moistened.

3. Turn dough out onto a lightly floured surface. Quickly knead by gently folding and pressing dough for 10 to 12 strokes or until nearly smooth. Pat or lightly roll dough to ½-inch thickness. Cut dough with a floured 2½-inch biscuit cutter, dipping the cutter into flour between cuts. Place biscuits 1 inch apart on an ungreased baking sheet.

4. Bake in a 450° oven for 10 to 12 minutes or until golden. Remove biscuits from baking sheet; cool slightly on a wire rack. If desired, drizzle with Lemon Glaze. Serve warm. *Makes 8 to 10 biscuits.*

Lemon Glaze: In a small bowl, stir together 1 cup sifted *powdered sugar,* 1 tablespoon *milk,* ½ teaspoon finely shredded *lemon peel,* and ¼ teaspoon *vanilla.* Stir in enough additional *milk, 1 teaspoon* at a time, to make a glaze of drizzling consistency.

Make-Ahead Tip: Prepare and bake Lemon Burst Biscuits as directed, except do not glaze. Place biscuits in a freezer container or bag and freeze for up to 3 months. To serve, wrap frozen biscuits in foil and bake in a 300° oven for 20 to 25 minutes or until warm. If desired, glaze as directed.

Hearty breakfasts were part of the holiday season in the big house on the plantation. Standard fare were beaten biscuits, often served with gravy. Unlike drop biscuits, beaten biscuits were kneaded or pounded with a mallet or iron rod. Cooks often timed the steady strokes of beating with the rhythm of a spiritual.

Cheesy Corn and Grits

Prep: 15 minutes • Bake: 45 minutes

1½ cups water
 1 teaspoon instant chicken bouillon granules
 ½ cup quick-cooking grits
 ½ cup shredded cheddar cheese (2 ounces)
 ¼ cup finely chopped green onions or fresh chives
 2 slightly beaten eggs
 1 8½-ounce can cream-style corn
 ½ cup milk
 ¼ cup shredded cheddar cheese (1 ounce)
    Fresh chives (optional)

1. In a medium saucepan, bring water and bouillon granules to boiling. Gradually stir in grits. Remove from heat. Cover and let stand for 5 minutes. Stir in the ½ cup cheese and the green onions. Stir in eggs, corn, and milk. Lightly grease a 1-quart casserole; transfer mixture to casserole.

2. Bake in a 350° oven for 45 to 50 minutes or until set in center. Sprinkle with the ¼ cup cheese. Let stand for 1 to 2 minutes or until cheese is melted. If desired, garnish with chives. *Makes 4 servings.*

Although considered a Southern classic, grits originally were a Native American food. The Indians developed the technique of making hominy from dried corn and grinding it into grits. This version is extra creamy because it's made with cream-style corn.

Cheesy Corn and Grits

Bacon Spoon Bread Soufflé
Prep: 25 minutes • Bake: 45 minutes

- 4 slices bacon
- 1 cup water
- ½ cup yellow cornmeal
- 1 cup shredded cheddar cheese (4 ounces)
- 1 8½-ounce can cream-style corn
- 2 tablespoons butter or margarine
- ¾ cup milk
- 3 egg yolks
- 1 teaspoon baking powder
- 3 egg whites

1. In a large skillet, cook bacon over medium heat until crisp. Drain and crumble bacon; set aside. Lightly grease a 1½-quart casserole; set aside.

2. In a medium saucepan, combine water and cornmeal. Bring to boiling; reduce heat.

Cook and stir about 1 minute or until very thick. Remove from heat. Add cheese, corn, and butter, stirring until cheese is melted and mixture is smooth. Stir in milk.

3. In a small bowl, beat egg yolks and baking powder until mixed. Stir into cornmeal mixture; stir in bacon.

4. In a medium bowl, beat egg whites with an electric mixer on medium speed until stiff peaks form (tips stand straight). Fold beaten egg whites into cornmeal mixture. Transfer mixture to prepared casserole.

5. Bake in a 325° oven for 45 to 50 minutes or until a knife inserted near center comes out clean. Serve immediately. *Makes 6 servings.*

In the 1847 book The Carolina Housewife, *by Sara Rutledge, spoon bread was described this way: "It has the appearance when cooked, of a baked batter pudding, and when rich, and well mixed, it has almost the delicacy of a baked custard." Serve this delicate dish with a spoon for your holiday breakfast.*

Cranberry-Walnut Muesli
Prep: 15 minutes • Chill: 8 hours

- 1½ cups regular rolled oats (not quick-cooking rolled oats)
- 1½ cups water
- 2 6-ounce cartons plain or fruit-flavored yogurt
- 1 medium mango, seeded, peeled, and cut into ½-inch pieces
- 1 medium banana, peeled and chopped
- ½ cup dried cranberries or golden raisins
- 3 tablespoons brown sugar
- 3 tablespoons toasted, coarsely chopped walnuts
- 1½ teaspoons finely shredded lemon peel
- ½ teaspoon vanilla

1. Place oats in a large bowl. Pour water over oats. Cover and refrigerate for at least 8 hours or up to 24 hours.

2. Before serving, stir yogurt, mango, banana, cranberries, brown sugar, walnuts, lemon peel, and vanilla into oat mixture. *Makes 6 servings.*

Muesli" is the *German word for "mixture." This appealing Swiss-style breakfast cereal, similar to granola, can contain any mixture of cereals, fruits, nuts, and seeds. Our yuletide version combines cranberries and other fruits with oats, yogurt, and walnuts.*

Baking Day

Baking bread these days is a luxury—a treat we share with our loved ones. During colonial times, it was a necessity. Cooks devoted one or two days a week to baking. They would heat the brick or stone oven for hours before adding the loaves. And, since heat could vary, they had to develop a sixth sense about timing. Thank goodness our ovens are more predictable. However, it still makes sense to do our holiday baking in a blitz, preparing our doughs and baking our loaves one right after another. And even though we have bread machines, fast-rising yeast, and accurate ovens, the thought behind baking bread for the people we care about hasn't changed one bit. Try some of the following recipes on your baking day.

Cardamom-Almond Wreaths (recipe, page 65)

Cranberry Bread Twist

2. Add milk mixture to flour mixture; add egg. Beat with an electric mixer on low to medium speed for 30 seconds, scraping side of bowl constantly. Beat on high speed for 3 minutes. Using a wooden spoon, stir in as much of the remaining flour as you can.

3. Turn dough out onto a lightly floured surface. Knead in enough of the remaining flour to make a moderately soft dough that is smooth and elastic (3 to 5 minutes total).

4. Shape into a ball. Place in a lightly greased bowl; turn once to grease surface. Cover; let rise in a warm place until double in size (1 to 1½ hours).

5. Meanwhile, for filling, in a small bowl, stir together cranberries, brown sugar, pecans, orange peel, cinnamon, nutmeg, and cloves; set aside.

6. Punch dough down. Turn out onto a lightly floured surface. Cover and let rest for 10 minutes.

7. Roll dough into a 14×10-inch rectangle. Brush with the melted butter. Spread filling onto dough. Starting from a long side, roll up into a spiral; seal seam. Cut roll in half lengthwise. Turn cut sides up. Loosely twist halves together, keeping the cut sides up. Pinch ends to seal.

8. Lightly grease a baking sheet. Place loaf on baking sheet. Cover and let rise in a warm place until nearly double in size (about 30 minutes).

9. Bake in a 375° oven about 25 minutes or until golden. Remove from baking sheet. Cool on a wire rack. Drizzle with Orange Glaze. *Makes 1 loaf.*

*C*hockful of cranberries, pecans, and spices, this sweet bread is reminiscent of a Danish pastry. Take it to work or serve it at a holiday breakfast or brunch.

Cranberry Bread Twist
Prep: 40 minutes • Rise: 1½ hours • Bake: 25 minutes

2¾ to 3 cups all-purpose flour
  1 package active dry yeast
  ½ cup milk
  ¼ cup water
  2 tablespoons granulated sugar
  2 tablespoons butter
  ½ teaspoon salt
  1 egg
  ½ cup finely chopped fresh cranberries
  ¼ cup packed brown sugar
  2 tablespoons finely chopped pecans
1½ teaspoons finely shredded orange peel
  ¼ teaspoon ground cinnamon
  ¼ teaspoon ground nutmeg
  ⅛ teaspoon ground cloves
1½ teaspoons butter, melted
  ½ recipe Orange Glaze (recipe, page 68)

1. In a large bowl, stir together *1 cup* of the flour and the yeast. In a small saucepan, heat and stir milk, water, granulated sugar, 2 tablespoons butter, and salt just until warm (120° to 130°) and butter is almost melted.

Sally Lunn Bread

Prep: 20 minutes • Rise: 1 hour 35 minutes • Bake: 40 minutes

- 3 cups all-purpose flour
- 1 package active dry yeast
- 1 cup milk
- 3 tablespoons sugar
- 3 tablespoons butter
- ½ teaspoon salt
- 2 slightly beaten eggs

1. In a large bowl, stir together *1½ cups* of the flour and the yeast. In a small saucepan, heat and stir milk, sugar, butter, and salt just until warm (120° to 130°) and butter is almost melted.

2. Using a wooden spoon, stir milk mixture into flour mixture; add eggs. Beat with an electric mixer on low to medium speed for 30 seconds, scraping side of bowl constantly. Beat on high speed for 3 minutes. Using a wooden spoon, stir in as much of the remaining flour as you can. Cover and let rise in a warm place until double in size (about 1 hour).

3. Lightly grease a 7- to 8-cup tube pan or Turk's head mold. Using a spoon, stir batter down. Spread batter evenly into prepared pan. Cover and let rise in a warm place until nearly double in size (about 35 minutes).

4. Bake in a 375° oven for 20 minutes. Cover with foil. Bake about 20 minutes more or until bread sounds hollow when tapped. Remove from pan. Cool on wire rack. Serve warm or cool. *Makes 1 loaf.*

Anadama Bread

Prep: 40 minutes • Rise: 1½ hours • Bake: 40 minutes

- 4½ to 5 cups all-purpose flour
- 2 packages active dry yeast
- 2 cups cold water
- 1 cup yellow cornmeal
- ½ cup molasses
- ⅓ cup shortening
- 2 teaspoons salt
- 2 eggs
- 2 tablespoons butter, melted

1. In a large bowl, stir together *1 cup* of the flour and the yeast. In a medium saucepan, combine water and cornmeal. Cook and stir until thickened and bubbly. Remove from heat. Stir in molasses, shortening, and salt. Cool just until warm (115° to 120°).

2. Add molasses mixture to flour mixture; add eggs. Beat with an electric mixer on low to medium speed for 30 seconds, scraping side of bowl constantly. Beat on high speed for 3 minutes. Using a wooden spoon, stir in as much of the remaining flour as you can.

3. Turn dough out onto a lightly floured surface. Knead in enough of the remaining flour to make a moderately stiff dough that is smooth and elastic (6 to 8 minutes total). Shape into a ball. Place in a lightly greased bowl; turn once. Cover and let rise in a warm place until double (about 1 hour).

4. Punch dough down. Turn out onto a lightly floured surface. Divide dough in half. Cover and let rest for 10 minutes.

5. Lightly grease two 8×4×2-inch loaf pans. Shape *each* dough portion into a loaf. Place in pans. Cover; let rise in a warm place until nearly double in size (about 30 minutes).

6. Brush with butter. Bake in a 375° oven about 40 minutes or until bread sounds hollow when lightly tapped, covering loosely with foil for the last 20 minutes of baking. Immediately remove from pans. Cool on wire racks. *Makes 2 loaves.*

The origins of Sally Lunn bread are uncertain. One story says the bread was named for an English girl who sold baked goods in the town of Bath. Another says the words "sun" and "moon" in French—"soleil" and "lune"—described the bread's brown top and white bottom. Whatever the origin, we do know this ring-shaped bread was served for tea in colonial times.

Anadama Bread

As the story goes, this bread was invented by a man whose wife didn't like to bake. In desperation, he baked his own bread while mumbling about his wife, Anna. He must have been a good baker, because his cornmeal-molasses bread remains a favorite.

Blueberry Sourdough Bread

Prep: 1 hour • Stand: 8 hours • Rise: 70 minutes • Bake: 25 minutes

  1 cup Sourdough Starter
  4 to 4½ cups all-purpose flour
  1 package active dry yeast
  1 cup milk
  3 tablespoons cooking oil
  1 tablespoon sugar
1½ teaspoons salt
  ½ teaspoon baking soda
  ½ cup dried blueberries, dried cherries, or raisins
  ½ cup chopped walnuts
  1 slightly beaten egg white
  1 tablespoon water

1. Bring Sourdough Starter to room temperature. In a large bowl, stir together 1¼ cups of the flour and the yeast. In a small saucepan, heat and stir milk, oil, sugar, and salt just until warm (120° to 130°).

2. Add milk mixture to flour mixture; add Sourdough Starter. Beat with an electric mixer on low speed for 30 seconds, scraping side of bowl constantly. Beat on high speed for 3 minutes. Combine *2 cups* of the remaining flour and the baking soda. Using a wooden spoon, stir flour mixture into yeast mixture until combined. Stir in berries and walnuts. Stir in as much of the remaining flour as you can.

3. Turn dough out onto a lightly floured surface. Knead in enough of the remaining flour to make a moderately stiff dough that is smooth and elastic (6 to 8 minutes total). Shape into a ball. Place in a lightly greased bowl; turn once to grease surface. Cover and let rise in a warm place until double in size (45 to 60 minutes).

4. Punch dough down. Turn out onto a lightly floured surface. Divide dough in half. Cover and let rest for 10 minutes.

5. Lightly grease 2 baking sheets. Shape *each* dough portion into a round loaf. Flatten each loaf to 7 inches in diameter. Place on baking sheets.

6. Using a sharp knife, make several crisscross cuts at right angles to each other across tops of loaves. Cover and let rise in a warm place until nearly double in size (25 to 30 minutes).

7. In a small bowl, combine egg white and water. Brush mixture onto loaves. Bake in a 375° oven for 25 to 30 minutes or until bread sounds hollow when lightly tapped. (If necessary to prevent overbrowning, cover loosely with foil for the last 10 minutes of baking.) Remove from baking sheets; cool on wire racks. *Makes 2 loaves.*

Sourdough Starter: In a large bowl, stir 2 packages *active dry yeast* into ½ cup *warm water* (105° to 115°); let stand 5 minutes to soften. Stir in 4 cups *all-purpose flour*, 3 cups *warm water* (105° to 115°), and 1 tablespoon *sugar*. Beat until smooth. Cover with 100%-cotton cheesecloth. Let stand in a warm place at least 8 hours or overnight. (The starter is then ready to use. It will look bubbly and clear liquid may rise to the top.) Stir before measuring. To store, pour remaining starter into a covered 2-quart or larger plastic container and refrigerate. *Makes about 5 cups.*

To use refrigerated starter, bring desired amount to room temperature.

To replenish starter, for every cup used, stir in ¾ cup *all-purpose flour,* ¾ cup *warm water* (105° to 115°), and 1 teaspoon *sugar.* Cover with 100%-cotton cheesecloth and let stand at room temperature for at least 8 hours or overnight. Cover and refrigerate for later use. *If starter isn't used within 10 days,* stir in 1 teaspoon *sugar.* Add 1 teaspoon *sugar* every 10 days unless replenished as above.

Cardamom-Almond Wreaths

Prep: 40 minutes • Rise: 2 hours • Bake: 20 minutes

¾ cup milk
⅓ cup butter, cut up
1 package active dry yeast
¼ cup warm water (105° to 115°)
3½ to 4 cups all-purpose flour
⅓ cup sugar
1 slightly beaten egg
¾ teaspoon salt
¾ teaspoon ground cardamom
1 8-ounce can almond paste
¼ cup sugar
2 egg yolks
1 tablespoon milk
   Dash ground cinnamon
3 tablespoons butter, melted

1. In a small saucepan, heat and stir the ¾ cup milk and the ⅓ cup butter just until warm and butter is almost melted. Cool to lukewarm (105° to 115°).

2. In a large bowl, stir yeast into warm water; let stand 5 minutes to soften. Using a wooden spoon, stir in the milk mixture, *1¾ cups* of the flour, the ⅓ cup sugar, the egg, salt, and cardamom until smooth. Stir in as much of the remaining flour as you can.

3. Turn dough out onto a lightly floured surface. Knead in enough of the remaining flour to make a moderately stiff dough that is smooth and elastic (6 to 8 minutes total). Shape into a ball. Place in a lightly greased bowl; turn once to grease surface. Cover and let rise in a warm place until double in size (about 1½ hours).

4. Punch dough down. Turn out onto a lightly floured surface. Divide dough in half. Cover; let rest for 10 minutes.

5. For filling, finely crumble almond paste into a large bowl. Add the ¼ cup sugar, egg yolks, the 1 tablespoon milk, and cinnamon. Beat with an electric mixer on low speed until mixture is combined (do not use higher speed or almond paste will spatter).

6. Roll *each* dough portion into a 12×9-inch rectangle. Spread *each* with *half* of the filling, spreading to within ½ inch of the edges. Starting from a long side of each, roll up into a spiral; seal seam. Cut rolls into ½-inch-thick slices.

7. Grease 2 baking sheets. Arrange *half* of the dough slices on *each* of the baking sheets in the shape of a wreath (about 9 inches wide), overlapping slices slightly. Brush tops of the wreaths with some of the melted butter. Cover and let rise in a warm place until nearly double (30 to 45 minutes).

8. Bake in a 350° oven for 20 to 25 minutes or until bread sounds hollow when lightly tapped. If necessary to prevent overbrowning, cover loosely with foil for the last 5 minutes of baking. Brush tops of wreaths with the remaining melted butter. Remove from baking sheets; cool on wire racks. *Makes 2 wreaths.*

*C*ardamom and almond paste or marzipan were two favorite Christmas baking ingredients of Scandinavian immigrants. Here the two meet in rich and flaky wreaths, perfect for morning coffee. You bake two—one to serve now and one to freeze or give away. Pictured on page 61.

Cardamom-Almond Wreaths

f you've ever seen an accordion in action—or made a paper fan—you'll have no trouble folding and shaping the dough for this breakfast or dessert bread. Mix and knead the dough by hand, or let your bread machine do the work.

Chocolate-Plum Accordion Bread

Prep: 40 minutes • Rise: 1¼ hours • Bake: 35 minutes

```
    4  cups bread flour
 1¼    teaspoons active dry yeast or bread
           machine yeast
    1  cup milk
    3  tablespoons sugar
    3  tablespoons water
    1  tablespoon butter
    1  teaspoon salt
    1  teaspoon ground cinnamon
    1  egg
 1⅓    cups pitted dried plums (prunes), snipped
    4  ounces bittersweet or semisweet
           chocolate, chopped
    2  long wooden skewers
```

1. In a large bowl, stir together *2 cups* of the flour and the yeast. In a small saucepan, heat and stir milk, sugar, water, butter, salt, and cinnamon just until warm (120° to 130°) and the butter is almost melted.

2. Add milk mixture to flour mixture; add egg. Beat with an electric mixer on low to medium speed for 30 seconds, scraping side of bowl constantly. Beat on high speed for 3 minutes. Using a wooden spoon, stir in as much of the remaining flour as you can.

3. Turn dough out onto a lightly floured surface. Knead in enough of the remaining flour to make a moderately soft dough that is smooth and elastic (3 to 5 minutes total). Shape dough into a ball. Place in a lightly greased bowl; turn once to grease surface. Cover and let rise in a warm place until double in size (45 to 60 minutes).

4. Punch dough down. Turn out onto a lightly floured surface. Cover and let rest for 10 minutes. Meanwhile, for filling, combine dried plums and chocolate.

5. Roll dough into a 15×10-inch rectangle. Sprinkle about *one-quarter* (about ½ cup) of the filling crosswise over 3 inches of dough along the short side of the dough rectangle. (It's very important to measure dough carefully during shaping.) Starting from opposite side, fold dough over filling, allowing dough to extend beyond filling-topped dough. Sprinkle another *one-quarter* of the filling on top of the filled layer, pressing filling lightly. Fold dough back over filling, accordion-style. Repeat filling and folding dough, accordion-style, twice more. Fold remaining dough over top, pressing lightly. (You'll have 5 layers of dough and 4 layers of filling.) Gently pat sides of dough to form a rectangle.

6. Lightly grease a baking sheet. Place loaf on the baking sheet. Cover and let rise in a warm place until nearly double in size (about 30 minutes).

7. Using a sharp knife, make a shallow lengthwise cut down center of the top layer, then make several crosswise cuts at 1-inch intervals. To keep bread layers from slipping while baking, insert wooden skewers (one close to each end of loaf) from top through bottom layer.

8. Bake in a 350° oven about 35 minutes or until bread sounds hollow when lightly tapped, covering with foil for the last 20 minutes of baking to prevent overbrowning. Remove from baking sheet; cool on a wire rack. Remove wooden skewers. *Makes 1 large loaf.*

Bread Machine Directions: Add the first 9 ingredients to the pan of a 2-pound bread machine according to the manufacturer's directions. Select the dough cycle. When cycle is complete, continue as directed starting with step 4.

Moravian Sugar Cake
Prep: 25 minutes • Rise: 2 hours • Bake: 20 minutes

- 1 small potato (about 5 ounces), peeled and cubed
- 1 package active dry yeast
- ⅓ cup granulated sugar
- ⅓ cup lard or shortening, melted
- 1½ teaspoons salt
- 3 to 3½ cups all-purpose flour
- 2 tablespoons butter
- ½ cup packed brown sugar
- ½ teaspoon ground cinnamon

1. Cook potato in 1 cup *boiling water* until tender. Cool to lukewarm (105° to 115°). Set aside ¼ cup of the cooking liquid. Mash potato in remaining cooking liquid, adding water if needed to make 1 cup mixture.

2. In a large bowl, stir yeast into reserved cooking liquid; let stand 5 minutes to soften. Stir potato mixture, granulated sugar, lard, and salt into yeast mixture. Stir in *1 cup* of the flour; beat well. Cover and let rise in a warm place until spongy (30 to 45 minutes).

3. Stir down. Using a wooden spoon, stir in as much of the remaining flour as you can. Turn out onto a lightly floured surface. Knead in enough of the remaining flour to make a moderately soft dough that is smooth and elastic (3 to 5 minutes total). Shape into a ball. Place in lightly greased bowl; turn once. Cover; let rise in a warm place until double (about 45 minutes).

4. Punch dough down; turn out onto lightly floured surface. Divide in half. Cover; let rest 10 minutes. Grease two 8×8×2-inch or 9×9×2-inch baking pans. Pat a dough portion into each prepared pan. Cover; let rise in warm place until nearly double in size (about 45 minutes).

5. With a wooden spoon handle or finger, make indentations in tops at 1½-inch intervals. Dot with butter. Mix brown sugar and cinnamon; sprinkle over dough. Bake in a 375° oven for 20 to 25 minutes or until golden. Serve warm. *Makes 2 cakes.*

Moravians were members of the Church of the Brethren, with roots in Bohemia, Moravia, and Poland. In the 1700s, they emigrated and settled in Pennsylvania, Georgia, and North Carolina. Moravians serve their Sugar Cake at candle teas held in early December. Considered to be the beginning of the Christmas season, the teas are held in Old Salem in the Brothers' House, where unmarried men lived during the early days of the settlement.

Chocolate-Plum Accordion Bread

Orange Bowknots

Orange Bowknots
Prep: 45 minutes • Rise: 1½ hours • Bake: 12 minutes

Dating back to a recipe that first appeared in the 1940s, this sweet and citrusy bread dough gets tied into tender pretzel-shaped rolls. Drizzle the glaze from a spoon or put it into a plastic bag, snip a small hole in the corner, and squeeze.

5¼ to 5¾ cups all-purpose flour
  1 package active dry yeast
1¼ cups milk
  ½ cup butter or shortening
  ⅓ cup sugar
  ½ teaspoon salt
  2 eggs
  2 tablespoons finely shredded orange peel
  ¼ cup orange juice
  1 recipe Orange Glaze

1. In a large bowl, stir together *2 cups* of the flour and the yeast. In a medium saucepan, heat and stir milk, butter, sugar, and salt just until warm (120° to 130°) and butter is almost melted.

2. Add milk mixture to flour mixture; add eggs. Beat with an electric mixer on low to medium speed for 30 seconds, scraping side of bowl constantly. Beat on high speed for 3 minutes. Using a wooden spoon, stir in the orange peel, orange juice, and as much of the remaining flour as you can.

3. Turn dough out onto a lightly floured surface. Knead in enough of the remaining flour to make a moderately soft dough that is smooth and elastic (3 to 5 minutes total).

Shape into a ball. Place in a lightly greased bowl; turn once. Cover and let rise in a warm place until double (about 1 hour).

4. Punch dough down. Turn out onto a lightly floured surface. Divide in half. Cover and let rest for 10 minutes.

5. Roll *each* dough portion into a 12×7-inch rectangle. Cut *each* rectangle into twelve 7-inch-long strips. Tie *each* strip loosely into a knot. Lightly grease 2 baking sheets; arrange knots 2 inches apart on baking sheets. Cover and let rise in warm place until nearly double in size (about 30 minutes).

6. Bake in a 400° oven about 12 minutes or until golden. Remove from baking sheets; cool on wire racks. Drizzle with Orange Glaze. *Makes 24 rolls.*

Orange Glaze: In a small bowl, stir together 1 cup sifted *powdered sugar* and 1 teaspoon finely shredded *orange peel.* Stir in enough *orange juice* (1 to 2 tablespoons) to make a glaze of drizzling consistency.

Snail's House Rolls

Prep: 45 minutes • Rise: 2 hours • Bake: 20 minutes

- 1 package active dry yeast
- ½ cup warm water (105° to 115°)
- 3¼ to 3¾ cups all-purpose flour
- 3 eggs
- ½ cup sugar
- ⅓ cup butter, melted and cooled
- ½ teaspoon salt
- 1 cup coarsely chopped almonds
- ¾ cup chopped candied orange peel
- ½ cup sugar
- ¼ cup butter, melted

1. In a large bowl, stir yeast into warm water; let stand 5 minutes to soften. Using a wooden spoon, stir in *1 cup* of the flour, the eggs, ½ cup sugar, the ⅓ cup melted butter, and the salt. Beat with an electric mixer on medium speed for 30 seconds, scraping side of bowl constantly. Beat on high speed for 3 minutes. Using a wooden spoon, stir in as much of the remaining flour as you can.

2. Turn dough out onto a lightly floured surface. Knead in enough of the remaining flour to make a moderately soft dough that is smooth and elastic (3 to 5 minutes total). Shape into a ball. Place in a lightly greased bowl, turning once to grease surface. Cover and let rise in a warm place until double in size (about 1½ hours).

3. Punch dough down. Turn out onto a lightly floured surface. Cover and let rest for 10 minutes.

4. For filling, in a small bowl, combine chopped almonds, candied orange peel, ½ cup sugar, and the ¼ cup melted butter.

5. Roll dough into an 18×10-inch rectangle. Brush with water. Spread filling over dough and press lightly. Starting from a long side, roll up into a spiral. Seal seam. Slice roll into 12 pieces. Lightly grease a 13×9×2-inch baking pan; place rolls, cut sides down, in prepared pan. Cover and let rise in a warm place until nearly double in size (30 to 45 minutes).

6. Bake in a 350° oven for 20 to 25 minutes or until golden. If necessary to prevent overbrowning, cover loosely with foil for the last 5 to 10 minutes of baking. Cool slightly in pan on a wire rack. Remove from pan. Serve warm. *Makes 12 rolls.*

These buttery-rich rolls came from the 1886 Kansas Home Cookbook. *It was the first fund-raising community cookbook designed to make money for "the friendless," illustrating that Christmas has long been a time to remember the poor.*

Snail's House Rolls

Apple Bread

Apple Bread
Prep: 30 minutes • Bake: 45 minutes

3 cups all-purpose flour
1 teaspoon baking soda
1 teaspoon salt
1 teaspoon ground cinnamon
¼ teaspoon baking powder
3 beaten eggs
3 cups shredded, peeled cooking apples
   (4 medium)
2 cups granulated sugar
⅔ cup cooking oil
1 teaspoon vanilla
   Powdered sugar (optional)

1. Grease and flour three 7½×3½×2-inch or two 8×4×2-inch loaf pans; set aside.

2. In a medium bowl, stir together flour, baking soda, salt, cinnamon, and baking powder; set aside.

3. In a large bowl, combine eggs, apples, granulated sugar, oil, and vanilla. Add flour mixture to egg mixture; stir just until moistened (batter should be lumpy). Evenly spoon batter into prepared pans.

4. Bake in a 325° oven for 45 to 55 minutes or until wooden toothpick inserted near centers comes out clean. Cool in pans on wire racks for 10 minutes. Remove from pans; cool on wire racks. Wrap and store overnight before slicing. If desired, sprinkle with powdered sugar. *Makes 2 or 3 loaves.*

Johnny Appleseed has received credit for introducing apples to the West, but he actually visited only a small part of the frontier. One of his namesakes, the Jonathan apple, is a good cooking apple to use in this bread. Other choices are the Jonagold, Newtown Pippin, Rome Beauty, Golden Delicious, and Granny Smith.

Pumpkin and Banana Bread
Prep: 20 minutes • Bake: 50 minutes

2¾ cups all-purpose flour
1½ cups granulated sugar
½ cup packed brown sugar
1 tablespoon baking powder
2 teaspoons pumpkin pie spice
½ teaspoon baking soda
¼ teaspoon salt
4 beaten eggs
1 cup canned pumpkin
1 cup mashed ripe banana
½ cup cooking oil
2 tablespoons lemon juice
1 cup chopped walnuts or pecans

1. Grease the bottoms and ½ inch up the sides of two 8×4×2-inch or 9×5×3-inch loaf pans; set aside.

2. In a very large bowl, stir together flour, granulated sugar, brown sugar, baking powder, pumpkin pie spice, baking soda, and salt. Make a well in the center of the flour mixture; set aside.

3. In a medium bowl, combine eggs, pumpkin, banana, oil, and lemon juice. Add egg mixture all at once to flour mixture. Stir just until moistened (batter should be lumpy). Fold in nuts. Evenly divide batter between prepared pans.

4. Bake in a 350° oven about 50 minutes or until a wooden toothpick inserted near centers comes out clean. Cool in pans on wire racks for 10 minutes. Remove from pans; cool on wire racks. Wrap and store overnight before slicing. *Makes 2 loaves.*

Pumpkin, an American staple since the time of the Pilgrims, was at first rejected as "peasant food." It soon appeared in some form on American tables almost every day. Over the years, inventive cooks have used pumpkin in everything from pies and puddings to cakes and breads, such as this pumpkin-banana combination.

Eggnog Bread

Eggnog Bread

Prep: 15 minutes • Bake: 45 minutes

E

ggnog became
a hit at Christmas
time in the South. In fact,
many Southerners still
keep a carton in the
refrigerator during the
holiday season. Not only
is eggnog delicious for
drinking, it also appears
in cookies, ice cream,
pies, and breads. You can
make this loaf with
refrigerated eggnog
during the holidays or use
shelf-stable canned
eggnog all year long.

2 cups all-purpose flour
1 cup sugar
2 teaspoons baking powder
¼ teaspoon salt
⅛ teaspoon ground nutmeg
1 beaten egg
1 cup dairy or canned eggnog
½ cup butter, melted and cooled slightly
1 teaspoon vanilla
½ teaspoon rum flavoring

1. Grease the bottom and ½ inch up the sides of a 9×5×3-inch loaf pan; set aside.

2. In a large bowl, stir together the flour, sugar, baking powder, salt, and nutmeg. Make a well in the center of the flour mixture; set aside.

3. In a medium bowl, combine the egg, eggnog, butter, vanilla, and rum flavoring. Add egg mixture all at once to the flour mixture. Stir just until moistened (batter should be lumpy). Evenly spoon batter into prepared pan.

4. Bake in a 350° oven for 45 to 50 minutes or until a wooden toothpick inserted near the center comes out clean. Cool in pan on a wire rack for 10 minutes. Remove from pan; cool on a wire rack. Wrap and store overnight before slicing. *Makes 1 loaf.*

Blue Corn Bread

Prep: 10 minutes • Bake: 20 minutes

    1   cup all-purpose flour
    1   cup blue or yellow cornmeal
    ¼   cup sugar
    1   tablespoon baking powder
    ½   teaspoon salt
    2   beaten eggs
    1   cup milk
    ¼   cup cooking oil

1. Grease the bottom and ½ inch up the sides of a 9×9×2-inch baking pan; set aside.

2. In a medium bowl, stir together flour, cornmeal, sugar, baking powder, and salt. Make a well in the center of the flour mixture; set aside.

3. In another medium bowl, combine eggs, milk, and oil. Add egg mixture all at once to flour mixture; stir just until moistened (do not overmix). Pour batter into prepared pan.

4. Bake in a 425° oven for 20 to 25 minutes or until a wooden toothpick inserted near the center comes out clean. Serve warm. *Makes 8 or 9 servings.*

Boston Brown Bread

Prep: 20 minutes • Cook: 2 hours

    ½   cup cornmeal
    ½   cup whole wheat flour
    ½   cup rye flour
    ½   teaspoon baking powder
    ¼   teaspoon baking soda
    ¼   teaspoon salt
    1   cup buttermilk
    ⅓   cup mild-flavored molasses
    2   tablespoons brown sugar
    1   tablespoon cooking oil
    ⅓   cup raisins or chopped walnuts, toasted

1. Generously grease the bottom and ½ inch up the sides of a 7½×3½×2-inch loaf pan; set aside.

2. In a large bowl, stir together cornmeal, whole wheat flour, rye flour, baking powder, baking soda, and salt; set aside.

3. In a medium bowl, combine buttermilk, molasses, brown sugar, and oil. Gradually add milk mixture to flour mixture, stirring just until combined. Stir in raisins.

4. Pour batter into prepared pan. Grease a piece of foil; place foil, greased side down, over the loaf pan. Tightly press foil around edges to seal.

5. Place loaf pan on a rack in a Dutch oven. Pour hot water into Dutch oven around loaf pan until water comes 1 inch up the sides of the loaf pan; cover. Bring water to boiling; reduce heat. Steam for 2 to 2¼ hours or until a wooden toothpick inserted near the center comes out clean, adding additional boiling water to Dutch oven occasionally to maintain water level.

6. Remove loaf pan from Dutch oven; remove foil. Cool in pan on a wire rack for 10 minutes. Remove bread from pan. Cool slightly on rack. Serve warm. *Makes 1 loaf.*

Blue Corn Bread gets its color and nutlike flavor from blue cornmeal. The Pueblo Indians believed the color blue to have medicinal properties, so foods containing blue cornmeal had special significance. They served blue corn bread at feast dances to celebrate Christmas Eve and the winter solstice.

Made with whole wheat flour, cornmeal, and rye flour, steamed Boston Brown Bread was frequently served with baked beans as part of the Puritans' Sabbath Day meal. Today, it makes a delicious tea bread, especially when slathered with cream cheese.

Cherry-Almond Mini Muffins

Prep: 20 minutes • Bake: 12 minutes

  2 cups all-purpose flour
  ½ cup granulated sugar
  2 teaspoons baking powder
  ¼ teaspoon salt
  2 beaten eggs
  ½ cup dairy sour cream
  ½ cup milk
  ¼ cup cooking oil
  ½ teaspoon finely shredded lemon peel
  ¼ teaspoon almond extract
  1 cup dried tart red cherries, finely snipped
  ½ cup chopped almonds
  1 recipe Lemon Glaze

1. Lightly grease thirty-six 1¾-inch muffin cups or line with miniature paper bake cups; set aside.

2. In a large bowl, stir together flour, granulated sugar, baking powder, and salt. Make a well in the center of the flour mixture; set aside.

3. In a medium bowl, combine eggs, sour cream, milk, oil, lemon peel, and almond extract. Add egg mixture all at once to flour mixture. Stir just until moistened (batter should be lumpy). Fold in dried cherries and almonds. Spoon batter into prepared muffin cups, filling each cup full.

4. Bake in a 400° oven for 12 to 15 minutes or until golden. Cool in muffin cups on a wire rack for 5 minutes. Remove from muffin cups. Brush with Lemon Glaze. Serve warm. *Makes 36 muffins.*

Lemon Glaze: In a small bowl, stir together ¾ cup sifted *powdered sugar* and 2 teaspoons *lemon juice*. Stir in enough *water* (2 to 3 teaspoons) to make a glaze of brushing consistency.

Nutty Choose-a-Fruit Muffins

Prep: 20 minutes • Bake: 20 minutes

  1 cup sugar
  ½ cup butter
  2 eggs
  1 cup dairy sour cream
  ½ teaspoon vanilla
  2 cups all-purpose flour
  1 teaspoon baking powder
  ½ teaspoon salt
  ½ teaspoon baking soda
  ½ teaspoon ground cinnamon, cardamom, or nutmeg
  ½ cup chopped nuts
  ½ cup fruit (such as snipped dates, dried apples, dried cherries, or dried cranberries; or coarsely chopped banana, apple, or fresh cranberries)

1. Lightly grease twelve 2½-inch muffin cups or line with paper bake cups; set aside.

2. In a large bowl, beat sugar and butter with electric mixer on medium speed until mixed. Beat in eggs, sour cream, and vanilla.

3. In a medium bowl, stir together flour, baking powder, salt, soda, and cinnamon; stir in nuts and fruit. Add flour mixture to butter mixture. Stir just until moistened (batter should be lumpy). Spoon into prepared muffin cups, filling each cup ⅔ full.

4. Bake in a 400° oven about 20 minutes or until golden. Cool in muffin cups on a wire rack for 5 minutes. Remove from muffin cups. Serve warm. *Makes about 16 muffins.*

Nutty Zucchini Muffins: Prepare Nutty Choose-a-Fruit Muffins as directed, except substitute ½ cup finely shredded *zucchini or carrot* for the fruit.

Back to front: Cherry-Almond
Mini Muffins and Cranberry-
Orange Biscuits

Cranberry-Orange Biscuits

Prep: 20 minutes • Bake: 10 minutes

   2 cups all-purpose flour
   1 tablespoon sugar
   1 tablespoon baking powder
   1 teaspoon finely shredded orange peel
   ¼ teaspoon salt
   ¼ teaspoon baking soda
   ½ cup shortening
   ½ cup dried cranberries, finely snipped
   1 8-ounce carton orange or vanilla yogurt

1. In a large bowl, stir together flour, sugar, baking powder, orange peel, salt, and baking soda. Using a pastry blender, cut in shortening until mixture resembles coarse crumbs. Add cranberries; toss until mixed. Make a well in center of the flour mixture. Add yogurt all at once to the flour mixture. Using a fork, stir just until moistened.

2. Turn dough out onto a lightly floured surface. Quickly knead dough by gently folding and pressing dough 10 to 12 strokes or until nearly smooth. Pat or lightly roll dough to ½ inch thickness. Cut dough with a floured 2½-inch biscuit cutter, dipping the cutter into flour between cuts. Place biscuits 1 inch apart on an ungreased baking sheet.

3. Bake in a 450° oven for 10 to 12 minutes or until golden. Remove from baking sheet. Serve warm. *Makes 10 biscuits.*

S hape up these tangy cranberry biscuits for the holidays by cutting them with star- or tree-shaped cookie cutters.

Clockwise from front: Lady Baltimore Cake (recipe, page 79)
Raspberry Marzipan Tart (recipe, page 83)
Wassail Bowl (recipe, page 95)

The Afternoon Call

In well-to-do circles of the early 1800s, ladies celebrated the holidays by donning their finest dresses and setting out lavish spreads of food and drink (especially drink), while gentlemen went from house to house, conveying their holiday wishes. In Baltimore, young men set out early, carrying lists and maps. (Any gentleman wishing to remain on a lady's social list dared not overlook her.) The Dutch initiated these open houses to celebrate New Year's Day, but the custom soon extended to the days following Christmas. The modest fare of earlier times gave way to showy displays of cakes and confectioneries, similar to the desserts in this chapter. Let them inspire you to open your heart and your doors to friends and family this season.

Our holidays often mean a whirlwind of pageants, concerts, and dances, such as the **classic** Nutcracker. *Invite friends over after the matinee or evening performance for a sweet moment together. Make one or all of the following or ask friends to bring a treat.*

Lady Baltimore Cake (recipe opposite)

Chocolate Charlotte (recipe, page 87)

Choose-a-Filling Tassies (recipe, page 84)

Holiday fruit plate

Eggnog (recipe, page 95)

Coffee with condiments

Apricot-Cherry Fruitcake

Apricot-Cherry Fruitcake

Prep: 30 minutes • Bake: 1 hour • Chill: 2 weeks

1½ cups all-purpose flour
½ teaspoon baking powder
¼ teaspoon baking soda
 1 teaspoon finely shredded orange peel
½ cup orange juice or apple juice
 2 tablespoons light-colored corn syrup
 1 teaspoon vanilla
¼ cup butter
¾ cup packed brown sugar
 2 eggs
¾ cup snipped dried apricots
½ cup dried cherries or raisins
½ cup pitted whole dates, snipped
½ cup chopped pecans or walnuts
   Bourbon or orange juice (¼ to ½ cup)
   Coarse sugar (optional)
   Orange peel curls (optional)

1. Grease and lightly flour an 8-inch fluted tube pan. (Or grease an 8×4×2-inch loaf pan. Line pan with parchment paper; grease paper.) Set aside.

2. In a medium bowl, stir together flour, baking powder, and baking soda; set aside. In a small bowl, stir together shredded orange peel, the ½ cup juice, the corn syrup, and vanilla.

3. In a large bowl, beat butter with an electric mixer on medium to high speed for 30 seconds. Add brown sugar; beat until combined. Add eggs, one at a time, beating well after each (batter may appear curdled).

4. Add flour mixture and juice mixture alternately to butter mixture, beating on low speed after each addition just until combined. Combine fruits and nuts; fold into batter. Pour into prepared pan.

5. Bake in a 300° oven about 1 hour for tube pan (about 1½ hours for loaf pan) or until a wooden toothpick inserted near center comes out clean. If necessary to prevent overbrowning, cover cake with foil for the last 15 to 30 minutes of baking.

6. Cool cake in tube pan on a wire rack for 10 minutes. Remove from pan; cool completely on wire rack. (Or completely cool the cake in loaf pan on wire rack; remove from pan.) Wrap cake in bourbon- or juice-moistened 100%-cotton cheesecloth. Overwrap in plastic wrap. Store in refrigerator for at least 2 weeks or up to 8 weeks to mellow flavors; remoisten cheesecloth every 3 days or as needed. If desired, to serve, sprinkle with coarse sugar and garnish with peel curls. *Makes 16 servings.*

Lady Baltimore Cake
Prep: 50 minutes • Stand: 2 hours • Bake: 30 minutes

½ cup golden raisins
8 dried figs, snipped (½ cup)
¼ cup brandy
2½ cups all-purpose flour
2 cups sugar
1 teaspoon baking powder
1 teaspoon finely shredded orange peel
½ teaspoon baking soda
⅛ teaspoon salt
1⅓ cups buttermilk
½ cup shortening or butter, softened
1 teaspoon vanilla
4 egg whites
1 recipe Meringue Frosting
¾ cup chopped pecans, toasted
⅓ cup finely chopped candied red and/or green
    cherries
¼ cup finely chopped candied pineapple or
    mixed candied fruits and peels

1. In a medium bowl, combine raisins, figs, and brandy; let stand at room temperature about 2 hours or until brandy is absorbed, stirring occasionally.

2. Grease and lightly flour three 8×1½-inch round baking pans; set aside.

3. In a large bowl, stir together flour, sugar, baking powder, orange peel, baking soda, and salt. Add buttermilk, shortening, and vanilla. Beat with an electric mixer on low speed for 30 seconds, scraping side of bowl. Beat on medium to high speed for 2 minutes, scraping bowl often. Add egg whites; beat for 2 minutes more, scraping bowl. Pour batter into prepared pans.

4. Bake in a 350° oven about 30 minutes or until a wooden toothpick inserted near centers comes out clean. Cool in pans on wire racks for 10 minutes. Remove cakes from pans; cool completely on wire racks.

5. For filling, stir about *1½ cups* of the Meringue Frosting, the pecans, and candied fruits into the raisin mixture.

6. To assemble, place a cake layer on a platter; spread *half* of the filling over top. Add another cake layer and the remaining filling. Top with the remaining cake layer. Frost top and side with the remaining frosting. Store frosted cake in the refrigerator and serve the same day it is made. *Makes 12 servings.*

Meringue Frosting: In the 2-quart top of a double boiler, combine 1½ cups *sugar,* ⅓ cup *cold water,* 2 *egg whites,* and ¼ teaspoon *cream of tartar.* Beat with an electric mixer on low speed for 30 seconds. Place over boiling water (upper pan should not touch water). Cook, beating constantly with the electric mixer on high speed, for 10 to 13 minutes or until an instant-read thermometer registers 160° when inserted into the mixture, stopping beater and quickly scraping both sides of pan every 5 minutes to prevent sticking. Remove from heat; add 1 teaspoon *vanilla.* Beat for 2 to 3 minutes more or until frosting is fluffy and holds soft peaks. *Makes 5 cups.*

Make-Ahead Tip: Bake and cool Lady Baltimore Cake as directed, except do not fill and frost. Place cake layers in freezer bags; freeze up to 3 months. Before serving, thaw at room temperature. Prepare Meringue Frosting and filling; fill and frost as directed.

The name may be a little misleading. This cake actually was created in Charleston, South Carolina, as a white, billowy fruit-layered cake. Lady Baltimore Cake was so named because it appeared in a 1906 novel, Lady Baltimore, *penned by Owen Wister. The Lord Baltimore Cake, a companion yellow cake, was created from the leftover egg yolks. Pictured on page 76 and on the cover.*

Eggnog Cake

Prep: 45 minutes • Bake: 25 minutes

Eggnog often is linked to a British drink, syllabub, which became popular as a New Year's Day toast in New York. However, the fact that syllabub contains no egg makes that connection a little weak. Instead, eggnog may originate from a German egg punch that's made with milk and wine.

2⅓ cups all-purpose flour
1 tablespoon baking powder
½ teaspoon ground nutmeg
¼ teaspoon salt
⅔ cup butter
1½ cups sugar
3 egg yolks
1 cup dairy or canned eggnog
3 egg whites
1 recipe Creamy Eggnog Frosting

1. Grease and lightly flour two 9×1½-inch or 8×1½-inch round baking pans; set aside.

2. In a medium bowl, stir together flour, baking powder, nutmeg, and salt; set aside.

3. In a large bowl, beat butter with an electric mixer on medium to high speed for 30 seconds. Add sugar; beat until combined. Add egg yolks, one at a time, beating well after each addition. Add flour mixture and eggnog alternately to beaten mixture, beating on low speed after each addition just until combined.

4. Wash beaters thoroughly. In a medium bowl, beat egg whites with an electric mixer on medium to high speed until stiff peaks form (tips stand straight). Gently fold beaten egg whites into the batter. Pour batter into prepared pans.

5. Bake in a 350° oven for 25 to 30 minutes for 9-inch pans (30 to 35 minutes for 8-inch pans) or until a wooden toothpick inserted near centers comes out clean. Cool in pans on wire racks for 10 minutes. Remove cakes from pans; cool completely on wire racks. Fill and frost with Creamy Eggnog Frosting. *Makes 12 servings.*

Creamy Eggnog Frosting: In a heavy, medium saucepan, combine 1 cup *sugar,* ¼ cup *all-purpose flour,* and ¼ teaspoon *ground nutmeg.* Add 1½ cups *dairy or canned eggnog.* Cook and stir over medium heat until thickened and bubbly. Remove from heat.

Gradually stir hot mixture into 3 beaten *egg yolks.* Return mixture to saucepan. Bring to a gentle boil; cook and stir for 2 minutes more. Remove from heat. Stir in 4 teaspoons *rum* (or 4 teaspoons *milk or dairy or canned eggnog* and ¼ teaspoon *rum extract).* Pour mixture into a bowl. Cover with plastic wrap. Cool to room temperature without stirring.

In a medium bowl, beat 1½ cups *butter* with an electric mixer on medium to high speed about 30 seconds or until fluffy. Add cooled eggnog mixture, *one-fourth* at a time, beating on low speed after each addition until smooth.

Make-Ahead Tip: Refrigerate frosted Eggnog Cake in a covered container for up to 3 days. (Or bake and cool cakes as directed, except do not fill and frost. Place cake layers in freezer bags and freeze up to 3 months. Before serving, thaw at room temperature. Prepare frosting; fill and frost cake as directed.)

Eggnog Cake

Ginger Pound Cake

Stand: 30 minutes • Prep: 40 minutes • Bake: 1 hour

- 1 cup butter
- 5 eggs
- 1 cup milk
- 3 cups all-purpose flour
- 1 teaspoon baking powder
- ¼ teaspoon baking soda
- ¼ teaspoon salt
- 2 cups granulated sugar
- ¾ cup packed brown sugar
- 2 teaspoons vanilla
- ½ cup finely chopped crystallized ginger
  (2.7-ounce jar)
- 2 tablespoons grated fresh ginger
- 1 recipe Citrus Topping (optional)

1. Let butter, eggs, and milk stand at room temperature for 30 minutes. Grease and lightly flour a 10-inch tube pan; set aside. In a medium bowl, stir together flour, baking powder, baking soda, and salt; set aside.

2. In a very large bowl, beat butter with an electric mixer on medium to high speed for 30 seconds. Gradually add the 2 cups granulated sugar and the brown sugar, beating until combined. Beat in vanilla. Add eggs, one at a time, beating for 1 minute after each addition and scraping side of bowl frequently.

3. Add flour mixture and milk alternately to butter mixture, beating on low to medium speed after each addition just until combined. Gently stir in crystallized ginger and fresh ginger. Pour batter into prepared pan.

4. Bake in a 350° oven for 60 to 70 minutes or until a wooden toothpick inserted near center comes out clean. Cool in pan on a wire rack for 10 minutes. Remove from pan; cool completely on wire rack.

5. To serve, place cake on a serving platter. If desired, spoon Citrus Topping over cake; drizzle with syrup. *Makes 16 servings.*

Ginger Pound Cake

Citrus Topping: In a medium saucepan, combine 1½ cups *sugar* and 1 cup *water*. Bring to boiling; reduce heat. Boil gently for 15 to 20 minutes or until mixture forms a thick syrup, stirring occasionally. Stir more often as syrup begins to thicken (you should have about 1 cup).

Meanwhile, thinly slice 3 *blood oranges or oranges* and 12 *kumquats;* discard ends and any seeds. Add fruit to syrup, stirring to coat. Return to boiling; reduce heat. Simmer, uncovered, about 5 minutes or just until fruit is tender, gently turning fruit in syrup several times. Using a slotted spoon, gently remove fruit from syrup. Continue to boil syrup, uncovered, for 10 to 15 minutes more or until reduced to ¾ cup. Cool about 15 minutes.

Make-Ahead Tip: Bake and cool Ginger Pound Cake as directed, except do not prepare fruit topping. Place cake in an airtight container or wrap in foil. Store at room temperature for up to 2 days. (Or freeze for up to 3 months. Before serving, thaw cake at room temperature.) Prepare and add Citrus Topping as directed.

Pound cakes were so named because the original recipes contained a pound each of butter, sugar, eggs, and flour. At Mount Vernon and in Williamsburg, pound cakes were studded with currants or fruit; in Tennessee, they contained blackberry jam; in Virginia, they had banana; in Texas, pecans; and in Kentucky, bourbon. This ginger variation is sure to please.

Apricot-Cranberry Tart

Apricot-Cranberry Tart
Prep: 30 minutes • Bake: 11 minutes + 35 minutes

s American as apple pie" is not just a saying, it's a testament to how our nation grew up with pie and tarts. Humble pastries bursting with seasonal fruits have graced our tables for centuries. Just as in the pioneer days, this winter tart relies on canned summer apricots and fresh or dried autumn cranberries.

1 15-ounce package (2 crusts) folded
   refrigerated unbaked piecrust
½ cup granulated sugar
3 tablespoons cornstarch
1½ teaspoons pumpkin pie spice
¼ teaspoon salt
3 15¼-ounce cans unpeeled apricot halves,
   drained and cut into halves
1 cup fresh cranberries or ½ cup dried
   cranberries
1 egg white
1 tablespoon milk
1 tablespoon coarse sugar

1. Let piecrust stand according to package directions. Line an ungreased 10-inch tart pan with a removable bottom with *one* of the piecrusts. Press pastry into fluted side of tart pan; trim edge. Line with a double thickness of foil. Bake in a 450° oven for 8 minutes. Remove foil. Bake for 3 to 4 minutes more or until set and dry. Remove from oven. Reduce oven temperature to 375°.

2. In a large bowl, combine granulated sugar, cornstarch, pumpkin pie spice, and salt. Stir in apricots and cranberries. Spoon into baked tart shell.

3. Place the remaining piecrust on a lightly floured surface. Cut with 1- and 2-inch star-shape cutters or other desired cutters to make about 20 shapes. In a small bowl, stir together egg white and milk. Brush egg white mixture onto pastry shapes; sprinkle with coarse sugar. Arrange pastry shapes on top of filled tart.

4. Bake in the 375° oven for 35 to 40 minutes or until pastry is golden and filling is bubbly. Cool on a wire rack.

5. Before serving, remove side of pan and transfer tart to a serving platter. *Makes 8 servings.*

Raspberry Marzipan Tart

Prep: 40 minutes • Bake: 30 minutes • Chill: 10 minutes

⅓ cup seedless raspberry jam
1 recipe Rich Tart Crust (recipe, page 27)
1 recipe Pistachio Marzipan
2 ounces semisweet chocolate, cut up
  Chopped unsalted pistachio nuts (optional)

1. Spread jam onto the bottom of the Rich Tart Crust. Spread Pistachio Marzipan evenly over the jam. Bake in a 350° oven for 30 to 35 minutes or until the filling is golden brown and firm when lightly touched. Cool in pan on a wire rack.

2. In a heavy, small saucepan, cook and stir chocolate over low heat until melted. Spread onto marzipan. If desired, garnish with pistachio nuts. Refrigerate tart about 10 minutes or until chocolate is set.

3. Before serving, remove side of tart pan and transfer tart to a serving platter. *Makes 12 servings.*

Pistachio Marzipan: In a food processor bowl or blender container, combine ⅔ cup *sugar*, ½ cup *slivered almonds*, and 3 tablespoons *all-purpose flour*. Cover and process or blend for 1 minute or until almonds are finely ground. Add ⅓ cup *butter* and 1 *egg*. Cover and process or blend until smooth. Add 1 *egg*, 1 teaspoon *vanilla*, and ½ teaspoon *almond extract*. Cover and process or blend until smooth. Add ⅓ cup *unsalted pistachio nuts*, chopped. Cover and process or blend with several on-off turns until combined.

Marzipan is a sweet almond paste introduced by Scandinavian settlers, who used it in fillings and candies. In fact, children of Danish descent still shape colored marzipan into candies for Christmas. Our marzipan variation blends pistachio nuts with the almonds. Pictured on page 76.

Coconut Cupcakes

Coconut Cupcakes

Prep: 20 minutes • Bake: 12 minutes

⅔ cup all-purpose flour
½ teaspoon baking powder
⅛ teaspoon baking soda
  Dash salt
¼ cup butter, softened
½ cup sugar
½ teaspoon vanilla
1 egg
¼ cup buttermilk
1 recipe Cream Cheese Frosting
1 cup flaked coconut

1. Grease and lightly flour twenty-four 1¾-inch muffin cups; set aside. In a small bowl, stir together flour, baking powder, baking soda, and salt; set aside.

2. In a medium bowl, beat butter with an electric mixer on medium to high speed for 30 seconds. Add sugar and vanilla. Beat about 2 minutes more or until light and fluffy, scraping bowl. Add egg; beat until combined.

3. Add flour mixture and buttermilk alternately to egg mixture, beating after each addition until combined.

4. Spoon about *1 rounded teaspoon* of the batter into *each* prepared muffin cup. Bake in a 350° oven about 12 minutes or until a wooden toothpick inserted in centers comes out clean. Cool in muffin cups on a wire rack for 5 minutes. Remove from muffin cups. Cool completely on wire rack.

5. Frost cupcakes with Cream Cheese Frosting. Sprinkle with coconut. *Makes 24 cupcakes.*

Cream Cheese Frosting: In a large bowl, beat 4 ounces softened *cream cheese* and 2 tablespoons *butter* with an electric mixer on medium to high speed until combined. Beat in 1 teaspoon *vanilla*. Gradually add 2½ cups sifted *powdered sugar*, beating until smooth.

A white Christmas in the South used to mean cooking with coconut, because December was the time coconuts appeared in the markets. Besides using coconut in their fruity ambrosia, Southerners liked to bake a round coconut snowball cake. Though these cupcakes are not as big, they'll have you dreaming of a white Christmas too.

Choose-a-Filling Tassies

Prep: 30 minutes • Chill: 1 hour • Bake: 25 minutes

½ cup butter
1 3-ounce package cream cheese
1 cup all-purpose flour
1 recipe desired filling (recipes below)

1. For pastry, in a medium bowl, beat butter and cream cheese with an electric mixer on medium to high speed for 30 seconds. Stir in flour until combined. Cover; refrigerate about 1 hour or until dough is easy to handle.

2. Divide chilled dough into 24 portions. Roll each portion into a ball. Press each ball evenly against the bottom and up the side of an ungreased 1¾-inch muffin cup. Fill *each* cup with *1 to 2 rounded teaspoons* of the desired filling.

3. Bake in a 325° oven for 25 to 30 minutes or until tops are light brown. Cool slightly (about 5 minutes) in pans on wire racks. Remove tassies from pans; cool completely on wire racks. *Makes 24 tassies.*

Almond-Raspberry Filling: In a medium bowl, beat 1 *egg*, ½ cup *sugar*, and ½ cup crumbled *almond paste* with an electric mixer on low speed until combined. Divide ¼ cup *red raspberry preserves* among pastry-lined muffin cups (about *½ teaspoon* each). Top each with *1 level teaspoon* of the almond paste mixture. Sprinkle with chopped, sliced *almonds*.

Apricot-Pecan Filling: Cover ⅓ cup finely snipped *dried apricots* with boiling water; let stand for 5 minutes. Drain well. In a medium bowl, combine 1 *egg*, ¾ cup packed *brown sugar*, and 1 tablespoon melted *butter*. Stir in ⅓ cup coarsely chopped *pecans* and the drained apricots.

Brownie-Nut Filling: In a heavy, small saucepan, cook and stir ½ cup *semisweet chocolate pieces* and 2 tablespoons *butter* over low heat until melted. Remove from heat. Stir in 1 beaten *egg*, ⅓ cup *sugar*, and

1 teaspoon *vanilla*. Place a whole *hazelnut (filbert)* or *peanut* in each pastry-lined muffin cup. Top each with *1 rounded teaspoon* of the chocolate mixture.

Cranberry-Nut Filling: In a medium bowl, combine 1 *egg*, ¾ cup packed *brown sugar*, 1 tablespoon melted *butter*, and 1 teaspoon *vanilla*. Stir in ⅓ cup finely chopped *fresh cranberries* and 3 tablespoons chopped *walnuts or pecans*.

Lemon Chess Filling: In a medium bowl, combine 1 *egg*, 1 *egg yolk*, ⅓ cup *sugar*, 2 tablespoons melted *butter*, 1 tablespoon *milk*, ½ teaspoon finely shredded *lemon peel*, 1 tablespoon *lemon juice*, and 1 teaspoon *cornmeal*.

Lemon-Coconut Filling: In a medium bowl, combine 2 *eggs*, ½ cup *sugar*, 2 tablespoons melted *butter*, ½ teaspoon finely shredded *lemon peel*, and 1 tablespoon *lemon juice*. Stir in ¼ cup *flaked coconut*.

Pecan Filling: In a medium bowl, combine 1 *egg*, ¾ cup packed *brown sugar*, 1 tablespoon melted *butter*, and 1 teaspoon *vanilla*. Stir in ⅔ cup coarsely chopped *pecans*.

Pumpkin Filling: In a medium bowl, combine 1 *egg*, ½ cup *canned pumpkin*, ¼ cup *sugar*, ¼ cup *milk*, and 1 teaspoon *pumpkin pie spice*.

Sherry-Almond Filling: In a medium bowl, combine ¾ cup *sugar*, 2 tablespoons *butter*, 1 tablespoon *all-purpose flour*, and ¼ teaspoon *ground nutmeg*. Stir in 2 beaten *eggs* and 2 tablespoons *cream sherry*; stir in ¾ cup ground *almonds*. Divide 2 tablespoons *strawberry or raspberry jam* among pastry-lined muffin cups (about ¼ teaspoon each). Top each with *2 rounded teaspoons* of the almond mixture.

Eggnog Cheesecake

Prep: 30 minutes • Bake: 50 minutes • Chill: 4 hours

- 1½ cups finely crushed vanilla wafers
- ⅛ teaspoon ground nutmeg
- ¼ cup butter, melted
- 2 8-ounce packages cream cheese, softened
- ½ cup sugar
- 2 teaspoons cornstarch
- 1 teaspoon vanilla
- ½ teaspoon ground nutmeg
- 3 eggs
- ¾ cup regular or reduced-fat dairy eggnog
- 2 tablespoons brandy or rum
- 1 recipe Brandied Cherry-Cranberry Sauce

1. For crust, in a small bowl, combine crushed vanilla wafers and the ⅛ teaspoon nutmeg. Stir in melted butter. Press crumb mixture onto the bottom and 1 to 1¼ inches up the side of an 8-inch springform pan; set aside.

2. For filling, in a large bowl, beat cream cheese, sugar, cornstarch, vanilla, and the ½ teaspoon nutmeg with an electric mixer on medium speed until combined. Add eggs; beat on low speed just until combined. Stir in eggnog and brandy. Pour into crust-lined pan. Place in a shallow baking pan in oven.

3. Bake in a 350° oven for 50 to 60 minutes or until center appears nearly set when shaken. Cool in pan on a wire rack for 15 minutes. Loosen crust from side of the pan; cool 30 minutes more. Remove side of the pan; cool cheesecake completely.

4. Cover and refrigerate for at least 4 hours or up to 24 hours. Before serving, spoon Brandied Cherry-Cranberry Sauce over cheesecake. *Makes 12 servings.*

Brandied Cherry-Cranberry Sauce: In a small saucepan, combine one 12-ounce jar (1 cup) *sweet cherry preserves* (not low-calorie) and 1 cup *fresh cranberries;* cook and stir over medium heat until preserves are melted and cranberries just start to pop. Remove from heat. Stir in 1 tablespoon *brandy or rum;* cool for 10 minutes. Serve warm or chilled. *Makes about 2 cups.*

Cheesecake rivals pie as America's best-loved dessert. First popularized by Lindy's Restaurant in New York, it now appears on holiday tables from coast to coast.

Eggnog Cheesecake

Chocolate Pecan Pie

Prep: 30 minutes • Bake: 1 hour

- 3 slightly beaten eggs
- ¾ cup light-colored corn syrup
- 3 tablespoons granulated sugar
- 3 tablespoons brown sugar
- 3 tablespoons butter or margarine, softened
- 1 teaspoon vanilla
- ⅛ teaspoon salt
- ½ cup finely chopped pecans
- ⅓ cup bourbon
- 1 cup semisweet chocolate pieces
- 1 recipe Cornmeal Pastry (recipe, page 28) or pastry for a single-crust pie
- 1½ cups pecan halves

1. For filling, in a large bowl, combine eggs, corn syrup, granulated sugar, brown sugar, butter, vanilla, and salt. Stir in chopped pecans and bourbon.

2. Pat chocolate pieces lightly onto bottom of unbaked Cornmeal Pastry shell. Place pastry shell on oven rack. Pour filling over chocolate. Arrange pecan halves on filling.

3. Bake in a 350° oven about 1 hour or until a knife inserted near the center comes out clean, covering edge of pie loosely with foil for the last 30 minutes of baking. Cool on wire rack. *Makes 10 servings.*

In the South, pecan pie competes with pumpkin for the status of number-one holiday pie. This version is accented with bourbon from the Bluegrass State, as well as chocolate. For the crust, try the Cornmeal Pastry on page 28, make your favorite 9-inch pastry, or start with a piecrust mix, a refrigerated unbaked piecrust, or a frozen deep-dish pastry shell.

Pear and Raspberry Trifle

2. In a small bowl, combine ⅓ *cup* of the pear poaching liquid and the brandy or 1 teaspoon vanilla.

3. In a 2-quart trifle dish or straight-sided glass serving bowl, arrange *one-third* of the ladyfingers. Sprinkle with *2 tablespoons* of the pear liquid mixture; dot with *about 2 tablespoons* of the preserves. Spread *about 1 cup* of the Egg Custard over the top. On top of the custard, arrange and fan out *3* of the cut pear halves. Sprinkle with ⅔ *cup* of the raspberries. Repeat layers 2 more times. Cover; refrigerate at least 3 hours or up to 4 hours.

4. Before serving, top trifle with remaining cut pear halves. Sprinkle with the remaining raspberries. In a chilled small bowl, beat whipping cream, sugar, and the ½ teaspoon vanilla with an electric mixer on medium speed until soft peaks form. Spoon whipped cream on top of trifle. If desired, garnish with mint. *Makes 8 to 10 servings.*

Poached Pears: In a large skillet, combine 1 cup *sweet white wine* (such as Sauternes or Riesling), ½ cup *sugar,* and 3 whole *star anise;* bring to boiling. Add 6 firm, ripe *pears,* peeled, halved lengthwise, and cored. Return to boiling; reduce heat. Cover; simmer for 10 to 15 minutes or until pears are tender. Using a slotted spoon, remove pears from skillet. Bring liquid in skillet to boiling; cook, uncovered, about 8 minutes or until reduced to 1⅓ cups. Remove star anise. Cover; refrigerate pears and liquid for at least 1 hour or up to 24 hours. *Makes 12 pear halves.*

Egg Custard: In a heavy, medium saucepan, combine 3 beaten *eggs,* 2 cups *half-and-half or light cream,* and ¼ cup *sugar;* cook and stir over medium heat just until mixture coats a metal spoon. Remove from heat. Stir in 1 teaspoon *vanilla.* Place saucepan in a sink of ice water and stir for 2 minutes. Pour into a bowl; cover surface with plastic wrap. Refrigerate for at least 1 hour or up to 24 hours. *Makes 2¾ cups.*

Pear and Raspberry Trifle

Prep: 1 hour • Chill: 4 hours

  1 recipe Poached Pears
  1 tablespoon pear, peach, or apple brandy or
       1 teaspoon vanilla
1½ 3-ounce packages ladyfingers, split in half
       lengthwise
  ½ cup seedless red raspberry preserves
  1 recipe Egg Custard
2¼ cups raspberries
  ½ cup whipping cream
  1 tablespoon sugar
  ½ teaspoon vanilla
      Fresh mint sprigs (optional)

1. Place Poached Pear halves, flat sides down, on a cutting board. Make 7 lengthwise cuts in each, starting about ½ inch from stem end and cutting to the bottom.

*T*he traditional English trifle relies on sherry for flavoring, which would have been an expensive import. So the ingenious Americans made do with their homemade fruit brandies or wines. For this trifle, you can poach the pears and cook the custard ahead of time, then assemble the whole dessert an hour or two before your open house.

Cranberry Fool

Start to finish: 15 minutes

1½ cups whipping cream
2 tablespoons sugar
1 teaspoon vanilla
1 16-ounce can whole cranberry sauce

1. In a chilled medium bowl, combine whipping cream, sugar, and vanilla. Beat with chilled beaters of an electric mixer on medium speed until soft peaks form.

2. Place cranberry sauce in a large bowl. Gently fold in whipped cream just until combined (the mixture should be red and white). Serve immediately or cover loosely and refrigerate up to 4 hours.

3. To serve, spoon mixture into sherbet dishes, parfait dishes, or wine glasses. *Makes 8 servings.*

"*F*ool" was a silly name given to an old English dessert of pureed fruit and cream. Because they were so simple to prepare, fools were very popular throughout the colonies. This version uses that New England favorite— the cranberry.

Chocolate Charlotte

Prep: 25 minutes • Cool: 45 minutes • Chill: 4 hours

1 envelope unflavored gelatin
4 ounces semisweet chocolate, chopped
⅓ cup whipping cream
8 to 10 ladyfingers, split in half lengthwise
1½ cups whipping cream
⅔ cup sifted powdered sugar
1½ teaspoons vanilla
  Unsweetened cocoa powder (optional)
  Whipped cream (optional)
  Shaved chocolate and/or white baking bar
    (optional)

1. In a small saucepan, combine unflavored gelatin and ¼ cup *cold water;* let stand for 5 minutes. Cook and stir over low heat until gelatin is dissolved; set aside.

Chocolate Charlotte

2. In a heavy, small saucepan, cook and stir chocolate and 3 tablespoons *water* over low heat until melted. Stir in the ⅓ cup cream until smooth. Stir in gelatin mixture. Remove from heat. Cool about 45 minutes or until room temperature, stirring occasionally.

3. Line a 1½-quart soufflé dish with plastic wrap. Carefully arrange ladyfinger halves, upright, around side of dish; set aside.

4. In a chilled large bowl, combine the 1½ cups whipping cream, the powdered sugar, and vanilla. Beat with chilled beaters of an electric mixer on medium speed until soft peaks form (tips curl).

5. Gently fold the cooled chocolate-gelatin mixture into whipped cream mixture. Spoon into ladyfinger-lined dish; spread top evenly. Cover and refrigerate for at least 4 hours or until set.

6. To serve, invert dish onto a serving platter; unmold charlotte. Carefully remove plastic wrap. If desired, sprinkle sides with cocoa powder; garnish with additional whipped cream and shaved chocolate. *Makes 6 to 8 servings.*

*D*uring Victorian times, dessert buffets featured decorated cakes, molded mousses, and gelatin desserts. Many were inspired by far-off places, such as the Charlotte Russe which alludes to a Russian influence.

Afternoon Tea

*Be ready for your
afternoon callers with
a tea that builds on our
British roots.*

*Gingerbread Scones
and/or
Cranberry-Pumpkin
Scones
(recipes opposite)*

*Pear and Raspberry Trifle
(recipe, page 86)*

*Apricot-Cherry Fruitcake
(recipe, page 78)*

*Short'nin' Bread
(recipe, page 93)*

Fresh strawberries

*Wassail
(recipe, page 95)*

Tea or coffee

Gingerbread Scones

Prep: 20 minutes • Bake: 12 minutes

  2 cups all-purpose flour
  3 tablespoons brown sugar
  2 teaspoons baking powder
  1 teaspoon ground ginger
  ½ teaspoon baking soda
  ½ teaspoon ground cinnamon
  ⅛ teaspoon salt
  ¼ cup butter
  1 beaten egg yolk
  ⅓ cup molasses
  ¼ cup milk
  1 slightly beaten egg white
     Coarse sugar (optional)
  1 recipe Nutmeg Whipped Cream (optional)

1. In a large bowl, stir together flour, brown sugar, baking powder, ginger, baking soda, cinnamon, and salt. Using a pastry blender, cut in butter until mixture resembles coarse crumbs. Make a well in the center of the flour mixture; set aside.

2. In a small bowl, combine egg yolk, molasses, and milk. Add egg yolk mixture all at once to flour mixture. Using a fork, stir just until moistened.

3. Turn dough out onto a lightly floured surface. Quickly knead dough for 10 to 12 strokes or until nearly smooth. Pat or lightly roll dough into a 9×7-inch rectangle. Cut into 8 rectangles. Place rectangles 1 inch apart on an ungreased baking sheet. Brush with egg white and, if desired, sprinkle with coarse sugar.

4. Bake in a 400° oven about 12 minutes or until bottoms are brown. Remove from baking sheet; cool slightly on a wire rack. Serve warm. If desired, serve with Nutmeg Whipped Cream. *Makes 8 scones.*

*From left to right:
Gingerbread Scones and
Cranberry-Pumpkin Scones*

Nutmeg Whipped Cream: In a chilled small bowl, combine ½ cup *whipping cream,* 1 tablespoon *sugar,* ¼ teaspoon finely shredded *orange peel,* ¼ teaspoon *vanilla,* and ⅛ teaspoon *ground nutmeg.* Beat with chilled beaters of an electric mixer on medium speed until soft peaks form (tips curl). Serve immediately or cover and refrigerate up to 2 hours. *Makes 1 cup.*

Make-Ahead Tip: Prepare and bake Gingerbread Scones as directed; cool. Wrap tightly in foil; place in a freezer bag. Freeze up to 3 months. Up to 2 hours ahead, prepare Nutmeg Whipped Cream; cover and refrigerate. To serve, reheat foil-wrapped frozen scones in a 300° oven for 15 to 20 minutes or until warm (if thawed, reheat for 10 to 15 minutes).

Cranberry-Pumpkin Scones

Prep: 20 minutes • Bake: 25 minutes

1¼ cups all-purpose flour
½   cup whole wheat flour
¼   cup granulated sugar
1   teaspoon baking powder
½   teaspoon baking soda
½   teaspoon ground cinnamon
½   teaspoon ground nutmeg
¼   cup butter, cut up
½   cup canned pumpkin
½   cup applesauce
⅓   cup chopped walnuts
⅓   cup dried cranberries
1   tablespoon brown sugar

1. In a large bowl, stir together all-purpose flour, whole wheat flour, granulated sugar, baking powder, baking soda, cinnamon, and nutmeg. Using a pastry blender, cut in butter until mixture resembles fine crumbs. Make a well in the center of the flour mixture; set aside.

2. In a medium bowl, combine pumpkin, applesauce, nuts, and cranberries. Add all at once to flour mixture. Using a fork, stir just until moistened.

3. Grease a baking sheet. Transfer dough to prepared baking sheet. Using floured hands, pat dough into an 8-inch circle. Cut into 8 wedges, but do not separate wedges. Sprinkle with brown sugar.

4. Bake in a 350° oven for 25 to 30 minutes or until brown. Remove from baking sheet; cool slightly on a wire rack. Cut again into wedges. Serve warm. *Makes 8 scones.*

Make-Ahead Tip: Prepare and bake Cranberry-Pumpkin Scones as directed; cool completely. Wrap tightly in foil; place in a freezer bag. Freeze up to 3 months. To serve, thaw at room temperature. Reheat foil-wrapped scones in a 350° oven for 10 to 15 minutes.

Caramel-Pecan Fudge

F udge is ever popular
at holiday time.
*This version boasts the
caramel-pecan flavor
of the praline, the famous
sweetheart of the New
Orleans French Quarter,
only it's a daintier size for
the dessert table.*

Caramel-Pecan Fudge

Prep: 25 minutes • Cook: 15 minutes • Stand: 40 minutes

1 cup granulated sugar
1 cup packed brown sugar
⅔ cup half-and-half or light cream
2 tablespoons butter
1 teaspoon vanilla
½ cup toasted chopped pecans

1. Line an 8×4×2-inch loaf pan with foil,
extending foil over edges of pan. Butter the
foil; set pan aside.

2. Butter side of a heavy 2-quart saucepan.
In the saucepan, combine granulated sugar,
brown sugar, and half-and-half. Cook and
stir over medium heat until mixture boils.
Clip a candy thermometer to side of pan.
Reduce heat to medium-low; continue
boiling at a moderate, steady rate, stirring
frequently, until thermometer registers 236°,
soft-ball stage (about 15 minutes). Adjust
heat as necessary to maintain a steady boil.

3. Remove saucepan from heat. Add butter
and vanilla, but do not stir. Cool, without
stirring, to 110° (about 40 minutes).

4. Remove thermometer from saucepan.
Using a clean wooden spoon, beat mixture
vigorously until fudge just begins to thicken.
Add pecans. Continue beating until fudge
becomes thick and just starts to lose its gloss
(about 10 minutes total).

5. Immediately spread fudge in the prepared
pan. Score into squares while warm. When
fudge is firm, use foil to lift it out of pan.
Cut fudge into squares. Store in a tightly
covered container for up to 1 week. *Makes
about 1¼ pounds (32 servings).*

A lmonds were
common culinary
*ground for many
immigrants. The British,
the Dutch, the Swedes,
the Norwegians, and the
Germans all brought their
treasured almond recipes
to America. Here,
almonds stand on their
own as a candied nut,
perfect for nibbling.*

Sugar-Roasted Almonds

Prep: 20 minutes • Cool: 30 minutes • Bake: 20 minutes

4 cups whole unblanched almonds or
mixed nuts
1 egg white
1 teaspoon water
⅓ cup granulated sugar
⅓ cup packed brown sugar
2 teaspoons ground cinnamon
½ teaspoon salt

1. Spread almonds in a single layer in a
15×10×1-inch baking pan. Bake in a
350° oven for 10 minutes. Remove from
oven; cool in pan for 30 minutes. Reduce
oven temperature to 325°.

2. In a large bowl, beat egg white and water
with a wire whisk or rotary beater until
frothy. Stir in granulated sugar, brown sugar,
cinnamon, and salt. Stir in cooled nuts.
Grease the 15×10×1-inch baking pan.
Spread nuts in single layer in prepared pan.

3. Bake in the 325° oven about 20 minutes
or until nuts appear dry, stirring once.
Transfer to waxed paper, separating into
individual pieces or small clusters to cool.
Store in a tightly covered container in the
refrigerator up to 1 week. *Makes 5½ cups.*

Bourbon Balls

Prep: 20 minutes • Stand: 30 minutes

    1 cup semisweet chocolate pieces
  ¼ cup sugar
    3 tablespoons light-colored corn syrup
  ⅓ cup bourbon
2½ cups finely crushed vanilla wafers
        (about 55 wafers)
  ½ cup finely chopped walnuts
      Coarse sugar, powdered sugar, and/or
        unsweetened cocoa powder

1. In a heavy, medium saucepan, cook and stir chocolate pieces over low heat until chocolate is melted. Remove from heat.

2. Stir in sugar and corn syrup. Add bourbon; stir until mixed. Add vanilla wafers and walnuts to chocolate mixture; stir until mixed. Let stand about 30 minutes.

3. Shape mixture into 1-inch balls. Roll in coarse sugar, powdered sugar, and/or cocoa powder to coat. Store in a tightly covered container up to 1 week. *Makes about 50 balls.*

Bourbon, first distilled in 1789 in Bourbon County, Kentucky, soon took the place of more expensive brandy in Southern cooking. In 1964, the United States Congress made it the only liquor to ever be designated as "a distinctive product of the United States."

Bourbon Balls

From top: Almond Short'nin' Bread, Chocolate-Dipped Cherry Short'nin' Bread, Pistachio-Topped Short'nin' Bread, and Lemon-Poppy Seed Short'nin' Bread (recipes opposite)

Short'nin' Bread
Prep: 20 minutes • Bake: 20 minutes

1¼ cups all-purpose flour
3 tablespoons granulated sugar or brown
        sugar
½ cup butter

1. In a medium bowl, stir together flour and sugar. Using a pastry blender, cut in butter until mixture resembles fine crumbs and starts to cling. Form the mixture into a ball and knead until smooth.

2. *For cut-outs,* on a lightly floured surface, roll dough to ⅜ to ½ inch thickness. Cut with 1½- to 2-inch cookie cutters into desired shapes; place 1 inch apart on ungreased cookie sheets. *For strips,* on a lightly floured surface, roll dough into an 8×6-inch rectangle. Cut with a knife into 2×1-inch strips; place 1 inch apart on ungreased cookie sheets. *For wedges,* on an ungreased cookie sheet, pat or roll the dough into an 8-inch circle. Using your fingers, press to make a scalloped edge. Cut circle into 16 wedges, but do not separate.

3. Bake cut-outs or strips in a 325° oven for 20 to 25 minutes or just until bottoms start to brown. (Bake wedges for 25 to 30 minutes or until center is set. Cut again into wedges. Cool on cookie sheet for 5 minutes.)

4. Remove cookies from cookie sheet; cool on wire racks. *Makes 16 to 24 cookies.*

Almond Short'nin' Bread: Prepare Short'nin' Bread as directed, except after cutting in butter, sprinkle mixture with ½ teaspoon *vanilla* and ½ teaspoon *almond extract.* Brush with *milk* and sprinkle with ¼ cup toasted, sliced *almonds* before baking.

Butter-Pecan Short'nin' Bread: Prepare Short'nin' Bread as directed, except use brown sugar instead of granulated sugar.

After cutting in butter, stir in 2 tablespoons finely chopped *pecans* and sprinkle with ½ teaspoon *vanilla.*

Chocolate-Dipped Cherry Short'nin' Bread: Prepare Short'nin' Bread as directed, except after cutting in butter, stir in ½ cup *maraschino cherries,* chopped and drained; 1 tablespoon *milk;* and 2 or 3 drops *red food coloring.* In a heavy, small saucepan, cook and stir ½ cup *semisweet chocolate pieces* and 2 teaspoons *shortening* over low heat until melted. Dip *half* of the baked and cooled cookies into melted chocolate; place on wire racks until set. In another small saucepan, cook and stir 3 ounces *vanilla-flavored candy coating* over low heat until melted. Dip remaining cookies into melted coating; place on wire racks until set.

Lemon-Poppy Seed Short'nin' Bread: Prepare Short'nin' Bread as directed, except stir 1 tablespoon *poppy seed* into flour mixture and add 1 teaspoon finely shredded *lemon peel* with the butter.

Oatmeal Short'nin' Bread: Prepare Short'nin' Bread as directed, except reduce flour to 1 cup. After cutting in butter, stir in ⅓ cup *quick-cooking rolled oats.*

Pistachio-Topped Short'nin' Bread: Prepare Short'nin' Bread as directed. In a heavy, small saucepan, cook and stir ½ cup *semisweet chocolate pieces* and 2 teaspoons *shortening* over low heat until melted. Drizzle chocolate onto cookies; sprinkle with toasted, chopped *pistachio nuts.*

Spiced Short'nin' Bread: Prepare Short'nin' Bread as directed, except use brown sugar instead of granulated sugar and stir ½ teaspoon *ground cinnamon,* ¼ teaspoon *ground ginger,* and ⅛ teaspoon *ground cloves* into the flour mixture.

*S*implicity at its purest describes the Southern adaptation of the beloved classic three-ingredient Scotch shortbread. In true American style, we added a few different ingredients to this simple holiday cookie to create a platter full of flavor options, perfect for an afternoon tea or a holiday open house.

steaming spiced fruit drink was a hit with gentleman callers on a cold day. This version contains no alcohol, so it was appropriate for the ladies to drink, an acceptable option during Prohibition, and now a beverage for the designated driver.

O

pen houses with their wine punches grew so popular that politicians started hosting receptions and inviting the public. In 1842, New York's Governor Seward, bowing to pressure from the Temperance League, substituted lemonade and cold water for wine punch at his New Year's Day reception. We're lucky that fruit-and-wine punches survived the politics of the day.

Apricot-Apple Sipper
Prep: 20 minutes • Chill: 8 hours

    4   cups apple juice or apple cider
    4   cups apricot nectar
    2   tablespoons honey
    2   tablespoons lemon juice
    4   inches stick cinnamon, broken
    1   teaspoon whole cloves
    1   teaspoon whole allspice

1. In a large saucepan, combine apple juice, apricot nectar, honey, and lemon juice.

2. For spice bag, place stick cinnamon, cloves, and allspice on a double-thick, 6-inch square of 100%-cotton cheesecloth. Bring corners together and tie with a clean string. Add the spice bag to juice mixture.

3. Bring to boiling; reduce heat. Cover and simmer for 10 minutes. Discard spice bag. Cool juice mixture. Cover and refrigerate at least 8 hours or overnight. Serve chilled in glasses. *Makes about 10 servings.*

Pineapple-Wine Punch
Start to finish: 10 minutes

    1   12-ounce can frozen pineapple-orange juice
          concentrate
    1   750-milliliter bottle dry white wine,
          chilled
    ¼   cup sugar
    ¼   cup lemon juice
    1   1-liter bottle ginger ale, chilled
          Ice cubes
          Fresh pineapple wedges (optional)
          Leaves from pineapple top (optional)

1. In a punch bowl, prepare pineapple-orange juice concentrate according to label directions.

2. Add chilled wine, sugar, and lemon juice; stir until sugar is dissolved. Slowly pour in ginger ale, stirring with an up-and-down motion. Serve over ice. If desired, garnish with pineapple wedges and leaves. *Makes about 25 servings.*

Pineapple-Wine Punch

Eggnog

Prep: 20 minutes • Chill: 4 hours

- 4 beaten egg yolks
- 2 cups milk
- ⅓ cup sugar
- 1 cup whipping cream
- 2 tablespoons light rum
- 2 tablespoons bourbon
- 1 teaspoon vanilla
- Whipped cream (optional)
- Ground nutmeg (optional)
- Pirouette cookies (optional)

1. In a heavy, large saucepan, combine egg yolks, milk, and sugar. Cook and stir over medium heat just until mixture coats a metal spoon. Remove from heat. Place the saucepan in a sink or bowl of ice water and stir for 2 minutes.

2. Stir in whipping cream, rum, bourbon, and vanilla. Cover and refrigerate for at least 4 hours or up to 24 hours. If desired, garnish with whipped cream, nutmeg, and cookies. *Makes about 7 servings.*

Low-Fat Eggnog: Prepare Eggnog as directed, except substitute 3 cups *fat-free half-and-half* for the milk and the whipping cream.

Chocolate Eggnog: Prepare Eggnog as directed, except stir in ¼ to ⅓ cup *chocolate-flavored syrup* with the rum.

Chocolate Eggnog and Eggnog

Peppermint Eggnog Punch: Prepare Eggnog as directed. Using 1 pint *peppermint ice cream,* reserve 2 scoops of ice cream in freezer. Place remaining ice cream in a chilled large bowl; stir until softened. Gradually stir in Eggnog and, if desired, ½ cup *rum.* Transfer to a punch bowl. Slowly add two chilled 12-ounce cans *ginger ale,* stirring with an up-and-down motion. Float reserved ice cream scoops on top. Serve immediately.

Up until World War II, eggnog parties prevailed in the nation's capital. Recipes for eggnog varied from the very rich bourbon version to those calling for different liquors. The variety continues today. This recipe offers a couple of flavor choices and even a low-fat option. The big change in making eggnog from the old days is that raw egg yolks no longer can be used for food safety reasons. That's why this recipe starts by cooking them in a custard first.

Wassail

Start to finish: 25 minutes

- 1 medium orange, halved
- 10 whole cloves
- 2 750-milliliter bottles claret or other dry red wine
- ½ cup sugar
- 4 inches stick cinnamon

1. Stud orange halves with cloves. In a large saucepan, combine orange halves, wine, sugar, and cinnamon.

2. Bring to boiling; reduce heat. Cover and simmer for 15 minutes. Remove orange halves and cinnamon. Transfer to a small heatproof punch bowl. Serve warm. *Makes about 12 servings.*

The term "wassail" used to refer to rowdy holiday revelers who expected a drink in return for their caroling. Now we think of wassail as a warm alcoholic punch, perfect for sipping at parties. Pictured on page 76.

Christmas Cookie Jar

To the British, they were biscuits. To the Dutch, they were *koekjes*. To us, they became cookies. And with each new group of immigrants, the American Christmas cookie jar grew fuller and fuller. The Germans brought their gingerbread favorites. The Norwegians shared their buttery gems. Over the years, we traded recipes and replaced hard-to-find European ingredients with those native to America—pecans, cranberries, cornmeal, maple syrup, and even bourbon. We love eating them, but we also love baking them with our families as a holiday tradition. Try decorating some of our American originals with your children this season. Then fill up your cookie jar and share.

Cranberry Pinwheels (recipe, page 100)
Mincemeat Swirls (recipe, page 104)
Spritz (recipe, page 105)

Maple Leaves

Maple Leaves

Prep: 45 minutes • Chill: 2 hours • Bake: 5 minutes per batch

In many areas of New England, maple syrup was the only sweetener available, so colonial cooks even figured out how to bake cookies with it. This modern version plays off the maple theme for the shape, but you can use any type of cookie cutter.

½ cup butter
¾ cup packed brown sugar
½ teaspoon baking soda
¼ teaspoon salt
1 egg
¼ cup pure maple syrup or maple-flavored syrup
1 teaspoon vanilla
¼ teaspoon maple flavoring
1 cup whole wheat flour
1¼ cups all-purpose flour
1 recipe Maple Frosting or raw brown sugar

1. In a medium bowl, beat butter with an electric mixer on medium to high speed for 30 seconds. Add brown sugar, baking soda, and salt. Beat until combined, scraping bowl. Beat in egg, maple syrup, vanilla, and maple flavoring until combined. Beat in whole wheat flour and as much of the all-purpose flour as you can with the mixer. Using a wooden spoon, stir in any remaining all-purpose flour. Divide dough in half. Cover and refrigerate about 2 hours or until easy to handle.

2. On a lightly floured surface, roll dough, half at a time, to ⅛ inch thickness. Cut with 2½- to 3-inch leaf-shape cookie cutters. On an ungreased cookie sheet, arrange cutouts 1 inch apart. If using raw brown sugar, sprinkle onto cookies.

3. Bake in a 375° oven for 5 to 7 minutes or until bottoms are light brown. Remove from cookie sheet; cool on a wire rack. If using frosting, frost cookies. *Makes about 48 cookies.*

Maple Frosting: In a medium bowl, beat ½ cup sifted *powdered sugar* and 2 tablespoons softened *butter* with an electric mixer on medium speed until combined. Beat in 3 tablespoons *pure maple syrup or maple-flavored syrup*. Beat in 1 cup additional sifted *powdered sugar*. Add additional pure *maple syrup or maple-flavored syrup, 1 teaspoon* at a time, to make a frosting of spreading consistency.

Make-Ahead Tip: Bake Maple Leaves as directed; cool completely. Do not frost. Place in a freezer container or bag and freeze for up to 1 month. To serve, thaw cookies and frost with Maple Frosting.

Gingerbread Cutouts
Prep: 40 minutes • Chill: 3 hours • Bake: 5 minutes per batch

½ cup shortening
½ cup sugar
1 teaspoon baking powder
1 teaspoon ground ginger
½ teaspoon baking soda
½ teaspoon ground cinnamon
½ teaspoon ground cloves
1 egg
½ cup molasses
1 tablespoon vinegar
2½ cups all-purpose flour
1 recipe Decorative Frosting (optional)
    (recipe, page 106)
   Currants (optional)
   Blanched almonds (optional)

1. In a large bowl, beat shortening with an electric mixer on medium to high speed for 30 seconds. Add sugar, baking powder, ginger, baking soda, cinnamon, and cloves. Beat until combined, scraping bowl. Beat in egg, molasses, and vinegar until combined. Beat in as much of the flour as you can with the mixer. Using a wooden spoon, stir in any remaining flour. Divide dough in half. Cover and refrigerate about 3 hours or until easy to handle.

2. Grease a cookie sheet; set aside. On a lightly floured surface, roll dough, half at a time, to ⅛ inch thickness. Cut with 2½- to 5-inch cookie cutters. On prepared cookie sheet, arrange cutouts 1 inch apart.

3. Bake in a 375° oven for 5 to 8 minutes or until edges are light brown. Cool on cookie sheet for 1 minute. Transfer cookies to a wire rack; cool. If desired, pipe on Decorative Frosting and decorate with currants and nuts. *Makes 20 to 48 cookies.*

Gingerbread Cutouts

Lemon Jumbles
Prep: 35 minutes • Chill: 1 hour • Bake: 8 minutes per batch

½ cup butter
1 cup granulated sugar
1 teaspoon cream of tartar
¼ teaspoon baking soda
1 egg
1 teaspoon finely shredded lemon peel
1 tablespoon lemon juice
1¾ cups all-purpose flour
   Coarse sugar

1. In a medium bowl, beat butter with an electric mixer on medium to high speed for 30 seconds. Add granulated sugar, cream of tartar, and baking soda. Beat until combined. Beat in egg, lemon peel, and lemon juice. Beat in as much of the flour as you can with the mixer. Using a wooden spoon, stir in any remaining flour. Divide dough in half. Cover and refrigerate for 1 to 2 hours or until easy to handle.

2. On a lightly floured surface, roll dough, half at a time, to ¼ inch thickness. Cut with a 2½-inch scalloped or round cutter. On an ungreased cookie sheet, arrange cutouts 1 inch apart. Sprinkle with coarse sugar.

3. Bake in a 375° oven for 8 to 10 minutes or until bottoms are light brown. Remove from cookie sheet; cool on a wire rack. *Makes about 36 cookies.*

Gingerbread Cutouts
Lemon Jumbles

Hermits

Prep: 25 minutes • Bake: 8 minutes per batch

- ¾ cup butter
- ¾ cup packed brown sugar
- 1 teaspoon ground cinnamon
- ½ teaspoon baking soda
- ¼ teaspoon ground cloves
- ¼ teaspoon ground nutmeg
- 1 egg
- ¼ cup strong brewed coffee, cooled
- 1½ cups all-purpose flour
- 2 cups raisins
- 1 cup chopped pecans

1. In large bowl, beat butter with electric mixer on medium to high speed for 30 seconds. Add brown sugar, cinnamon, baking soda, cloves, and nutmeg. Beat until combined, scraping bowl. Beat in egg and cooled coffee. Beat in as much of the flour as you can with the mixer. Using a wooden spoon, stir in any remaining flour. Stir in raisins and pecans.

2. Drop the cookie dough by rounded tablespoons 2 inches apart onto an ungreased cookie sheet.

3. Bake in a 375° oven for 8 to 10 minutes or until edges are light brown. Remove from cookie sheet; cool on a wire rack. *Makes about 48 cookies.*

Cranberry Pinwheels

Prep: 45 minutes • Chill: 3 hours • Bake: 8 minutes per batch

- 1 cup fresh cranberries
- ¼ cup orange marmalade
- 1 tablespoon honey
- ⅔ cup butter
- ½ cup granulated sugar
- 1 teaspoon baking powder
- 1 egg
- 1 tablespoon milk
- 1 teaspoon vanilla
- ½ teaspoon finely shredded orange peel
- 2 cups all-purpose flour
  Powdered sugar (optional)

1. For filling, in a covered medium saucepan, cook cranberries, marmalade, and honey over low heat until mixture boils and berries pop. Cook, uncovered, about 8 minutes more or until mixture is the consistency of thick jam, stirring occasionally. Remove from heat; cool.

2. In a medium bowl, beat butter with an electric mixer on medium to high speed for 30 seconds. Add granulated sugar and baking powder. Beat until combined, scraping bowl. Beat in egg, milk, vanilla, and orange peel. Beat in as much of the flour as you can with the mixer. Using a wooden spoon, stir in any remaining flour. Divide dough in half. Cover and refrigerate about 3 hours or until easy to handle.

3. On a lightly floured surface, roll dough, half at a time, into a 10-inch square. Cut into 2½-inch squares. On an ungreased cookie sheet, arrange squares 2 inches apart. Cut 1-inch-long slits from each corner toward the center of each square. Spoon ¾ *teaspoon* of the filling into center of *each* square. Fold every other tip to center to form a pinwheel, pressing lightly to seal tips. (If necessary to seal, lightly moisten tips with water.)

4. Bake in a 375° oven for 8 to 10 minutes or until edges are light brown. Remove from cookie sheet; cool on a wire rack. If desired, sprinkle with powdered sugar. *Makes 32 cookies.*

Giant Snickerdoodles

Giant Snickerdoodles

Prep: 20 minutes • Chill: 4 hours • Bake: 12 minutes per batch

4½ cups all-purpose flour
 2 teaspoons baking powder
 1 teaspoon baking soda
 ¾ teaspoon salt
 ½ cup sugar
 2 tablespoons ground cinnamon
1¼ cups shortening
 2 cups sugar
 2 eggs
1½ teaspoons vanilla
 ½ teaspoon lemon extract or 1 teaspoon finely
      shredded lemon peel
 1 cup buttermilk

1. In a medium bowl, stir together flour, baking powder, baking soda, and salt; set aside. In a small bowl, combine the ½ cup sugar and the cinnamon; set aside.

2. In a large bowl, beat shortening with an electric mixer on medium to high speed for 30 seconds. Add the 2 cups sugar. Beat until combined, scraping bowl. Beat in eggs, one at a time, beating well after each addition. Beat in vanilla and lemon extract or peel.

3. Add flour mixture and buttermilk alternately to shortening mixture, beating on low speed after each addition until combined. Cover and refrigerate about 4 hours or until easy to shape.

4. Lightly grease a cookie sheet; set aside. For each cookie, scoop dough using a ¼-cup measure or ¼-cup ice cream scoop. Roll each scoop of dough in the sugar-cinnamon mixture to coat. On the prepared cookie sheet, arrange balls 3 inches apart. Using the palm of your hand, gently press each cookie to ½ inch thickness.

5. Bake in a 375° oven for 12 to 14 minutes or until bottoms are light brown. Remove from cookie sheet; cool on a wire rack. *Makes about 24 cookies.*

Test Kitchen Tip: If using an ice-cream scoop, lightly coat the scoop with nonstick cooking spray to help prevent dough from sticking.

We wish we could explain why these crinkly-topped sugar cookies are called snickerdoodles, but that story's been lost over the years. We can tell you that the crinkly tops come from using a little more leavening than normal, which causes the cookies to rise, then fall. These big cookies need room to expand, so plan on five or six on a large cookie sheet. They brown more evenly if you bake one sheet at a time.

Moravian Christmas Cookies

Moravian Christmas Cookies
Prep: 40 minutes • Chill: 1 hour • Bake: 5 minutes per batch

½ cup molasses
¼ cup packed dark brown sugar
¼ cup butter, melted
1½ cups all-purpose flour
½ teaspoon ground cinnamon
¼ teaspoon baking soda
¼ teaspoon ground ginger
¼ teaspoon ground cloves
¼ teaspoon pepper
⅛ teaspoon dry mustard
⅛ teaspoon ground allspice

1. In a large bowl, stir together molasses, brown sugar, and melted butter. Add flour, cinnamon, baking soda, ginger, cloves, pepper, mustard, and allspice; stir until mixed. Divide dough in half. Cover and refrigerate for 1 to 2 hours or until easy to handle.

2. Grease a cookie sheet; set aside. On a lightly floured surface, roll dough to ¹⁄₁₆ inch thickness. Cut with a 2-inch scalloped or round cookie cutter. On the prepared cookie sheet, arrange cutouts 1 inch apart.

3. Bake in a 375° oven for 5 to 6 minutes or until edges are light brown. Remove from cookie sheet; cool on a wire rack. *Makes about 66 cookies.*

*T*hese spicy cookies are popular with Moravian children at the Love Feasts in Bethlehem, Pennsylvania, and Old Salem, North Carolina. A love feast is a musical holiday church service during which the congregation shares simple foods, such as these cookies, special buns, coffee, and hot chocolate.

Honey-Fruit Gingerbread (Lebkuchen)
Prep: 35 minutes • Bake: 8 minutes per batch

    1   egg
    ¾   cup packed brown sugar
    ½   cup honey
    ½   cup molasses
    3½ cups all-purpose flour
    1   teaspoon ground cinnamon
    ½   teaspoon baking soda
    ½   teaspoon ground cloves
    ½   teaspoon ground ginger
    ¼   teaspoon ground cardamom
    ½   cup chopped almonds
    ½   cup finely chopped mixed candied fruits and
        peels
    1   recipe Buttery Lemon Glaze
        Cut-up mixed candied fruits and peels

1. In a small bowl, beat egg with an electric mixer on high speed for 1 minute. Add brown sugar; beat on medium speed until light and fluffy. Beat in honey and molasses until combined. Set aside.

2. In a large bowl, stir together flour, cinnamon, baking soda, cloves, ginger, and cardamom. Add egg mixture. Using a wooden spoon, stir until combined (dough will be stiff). Stir in almonds and candied fruits and peels. Divide dough in half.

3. Lightly grease a cookie sheet; set aside. On a lightly floured surface, roll dough, half at a time, to a 12×8-inch rectangle. Cut into 2-inch squares. On the prepared cookie sheet, arrange squares 1 inch apart.

4. Bake in a 350° oven for 8 to 10 minutes or until edges are light brown. Cool on cookie sheet for 1 minute. Transfer cookies to a wire rack over waxed paper.

5. While cookies are still warm, brush with Buttery Lemon Glaze. Garnish with additional candied fruits and peels. Let glaze dry. Place in a tightly covered container and store for at least 8 hours or up to 7 days to soften. *Makes 48 cookies.*

Buttery Lemon Glaze: In a small bowl, stir together 1½ cups sifted *powdered sugar,* 1 tablespoon melted *butter,* and 1 tablespoon *lemon juice.* Stir in enough *water* (3 to 4 teaspoons) to make of drizzling consistency.

Honey, molasses, and spices flavor these sturdy German Christmas cookies, a favorite of the Pennsylvania Dutch. Women used to borrow each other's cutters to make an array of shapes: hearts, stags, or even hatchet-bearing Indians.

Honey-Fruit Gingerbread

Apees
Prep: 30 minutes • Chill: 1 hour • Bake: 6 minutes per batch

    1   cup butter
    1   cup sifted powdered sugar
    2   tablespoons dry white wine or apple juice
    1   teaspoon vanilla or rosewater
    ½   teaspoon caraway seed
    ¼   teaspoon ground nutmeg
    2   cups all-purpose flour
        Powdered sugar

1. In a large bowl, beat butter with an electric mixer on medium to high speed for 30 seconds. Add the 1 cup powdered sugar. Beat until fluffy, scraping bowl. Add wine, vanilla, caraway seed, and nutmeg; beat on low speed just until combined. Beat in as much of the flour as you can with the mixer. Using a wooden spoon, stir in any remaining flour. If necessary, cover and chill dough about 1 hour or until easy to handle.

2. Roll dough into 1-inch balls; roll in additional powdered sugar. On an ungreased cookie sheet, arrange balls 2 inches apart. Using a cookie stamp or the bottom of a glass, press each ball to about 1¾ inches in diameter. If necessary, use a pastry brush to brush out sugar that collects in the indentations of the cookie stamp.

3. Bake in a 375° oven for 6 to 8 minutes or until bottoms are light brown (the tops of the cookies should be pale). Remove from cookie sheet; cool on a wire rack. *Makes about 40 cookies.*

These Pennsylvania Dutch Christmas favorites are named after Ann Page, a 19th-century Philadelphia cook. (They're also called APs, apeas, apease, epise, or epees.) Ann was so proud of her cookies, she carved her initials on them. If you'd rather not sign your cookies, imprint them with any cookie stamp—they'll hold the design well, even after baking.

Pepper Nuts (Pfeffernuesse)
Prep: 30 minutes • Chill: 1 hour • Bake: 10 minutes per batch

⅓ cup molasses
¼ cup butter
2 cups all-purpose flour
¼ cup packed brown sugar
¾ teaspoon ground cinnamon
½ teaspoon baking soda
¼ teaspoon ground cardamom
¼ teaspoon ground allspice
⅛ teaspoon pepper
1 slightly beaten egg

1. In a large saucepan, combine molasses and butter. Cook and stir over low heat until butter is melted. Pour into a large bowl; cool to room temperature.

2. In a medium bowl, stir together flour, brown sugar, cinnamon, baking soda, cardamom, allspice, and pepper. Set aside.

3. Stir egg into molasses mixture. Gradually stir in flour mixture until combined, kneading in the last of the flour mixture by hand, if necessary. Cover and refrigerate about 1 hour or until easy to handle.

4. Divide dough into 12 portions. On a lightly floured surface, roll each portion into a 10-inch rope. Cut ropes into ½-inch pieces. Place ½ inch apart in an ungreased shallow baking pan.

5. Bake in a 350° oven about 10 minutes or until edges are firm and bottoms are light brown. Remove from pan; cool on paper towels. *Makes about 240 small cookies.*

Mincemeat Swirls
Prep: 30 minutes • Chill: 4½ hours • Bake: 8 minutes per batch

2 cups all-purpose flour
½ teaspoon baking powder
¼ teaspoon baking soda
½ cup shortening
1 cup packed brown sugar
1 egg
½ teaspoon vanilla
1½ cups prepared mincemeat
½ cup finely chopped nuts
1 teaspoon finely shredded lemon peel or orange peel

1. In a medium bowl, stir together flour, baking powder, and baking soda; set aside.

2. In a large bowl, beat shortening with an electric mixer on medium to high speed for 30 seconds. Add brown sugar. Beat until fluffy, scraping bowl. Beat in egg and vanilla. Add flour mixture to shortening mixture. Beat on low speed until combined. Divide dough in half. Cover and refrigerate for 30 minutes or until easy to handle.

3. Meanwhile, for filling, stir together mincemeat, nuts, and lemon peel; set aside.

4. Between 2 sheets of waxed paper, roll half of the dough into a 12×8-inch rectangle. Remove top sheet of waxed paper. Spread *half* of the filling over dough. Starting from a short side, roll up into a spiral, removing waxed paper as you roll. Moisten and pinch edge to seal. Repeat with remaining dough and remaining filling. Wrap each roll in plastic wrap. Refrigerate for at least 4 hours or up to 48 hours.

5. Grease a cookie sheet. Cut dough into ¼-inch-thick slices. On prepared cookie sheet, arrange slices 2 inches apart.

6. Bake in a 350° oven for 8 to 10 minutes or until edges are firm and bottoms are light brown. Remove from cookie sheet; cool on a wire rack. *Makes about 60 cookies.*

Spritz

Prep: 30 minutes • Bake: 8 minutes per batch

1½ cups butter
  1 cup granulated sugar
  1 teaspoon baking powder
  1 egg
  1 teaspoon vanilla
  ¼ teaspoon almond extract (optional)
3½ cups all-purpose flour
     Colored sugar or powdered sugar (optional)

1. In a large bowl, beat butter with an electric mixer for 30 seconds. Add sugar and baking powder. Beat until combined, scraping bowl. Beat in egg, vanilla, and, if desired, almond extract. Beat in as much of the flour as you can with the mixer. Using a wooden spoon, stir in any remaining flour.

2. Push unchilled dough through a cookie press onto an ungreased cookie sheet. If using colored sugar, sprinkle on cookies.

3. Bake in a 375° oven for 8 to 10 minutes or until edges are firm but not brown. Remove from cookie sheet; cool on a wire rack. If using powdered sugar, sprinkle on cookies. *Makes about 84 cookies.*

Chocolate Spritz: Prepare Spritz as directed, except reduce flour to 3¼ cups and add ¼ cup *unsweetened cocoa powder* with the granulated sugar.

You'll need a cookie press with different plates to make the shapes pictured on page 97. Then decorate these buttery German favorites with either colored or powdered sugar.

Bourbon Snaps

Prep: 45 minutes • Bake: 5 minutes per batch

½ cup packed brown sugar
⅓ cup butter, melted
¼ cup molasses
  1 tablespoon bourbon
¾ cup all-purpose flour
½ teaspoon ground ginger
     Whipped cream (optional)

1. Line a large cookie sheet with foil. Grease the foil. Set cookie sheet aside.

2. In a medium bowl, stir together brown sugar, butter, molasses, and bourbon. Stir in flour and ginger until combined.

3. Drop batter by level teaspoons 5 inches apart on the prepared cookie sheet. (Drop only 4 or 5 at a time.)

4. Bake in a 350° oven for 5 to 7 minutes or until bubbly and deep golden brown.

5. Cool cookies on cookie sheet for 1 to 2 minutes or until set. Quickly remove a cookie; roll cookie around a metal cone (for cone shape) or the greased handle of a wooden spoon (for a log shape).

6. When cookie is firm, slide off cone or handle and cool on a wire rack. Repeat with remaining cookies, one at a time. (If cookies harden before you can shape them, reheat about 1 minute or until softened.) If desired, fill cones with whipped cream. *Makes about 56 cookies.*

Bourbon Snaps

Sugar Cookie Cutouts

Sugar Cookie Cutouts

Prep: 1 hour • Chill: 30 minutes
Bake: 7 minutes per batch

⅓ cup butter, softened
⅓ cup shortening
¾ cup granulated sugar
1 teaspoon baking powder
   Dash salt
1 egg
1 tablespoon milk
1 teaspoon vanilla
2 cups all-purpose flour
1 recipe Powdered Sugar Icing
   Coarse and/or colored sugar
1 recipe Decorative Frosting
   Small decorative candies

1. In a medium bowl, beat butter and shortening with an electric mixer on medium to high speed for 30 seconds. Add granulated sugar, baking powder, and salt. Beat until combined, scraping bowl. Beat in egg, milk, and vanilla until combined. Beat in as much of the flour as you can with the mixer. Using a wooden spoon, stir in any remaining flour. Divide dough in half. Cover and refrigerate about 3o minutes or until easy to handle.

2. On a lightly floured surface, roll dough, half at a time, to ⅛ inch thickness. Cut with 2½-inch cookie cutters. On an ungreased cookie sheet, arrange cutouts 1 inch apart.

3. Bake in a 375° oven for 7 to 8 minutes or until edges are firm and bottoms are very light brown. Remove from cookie sheet; cool on a wire rack.

4. To decorate, spread cookies with white or tinted Powdered Sugar Icing. Sprinkle with coarse sugar. Let icing dry. Pipe cookies with white or tinted Decorative Frosting. Decorate with candies. *Makes 36 to 48 cookies.*

Powdered Sugar Icing: In a medium bowl, combine 4 cups sifted *powdered sugar* and ¼ cup *milk*. Stir in enough additional *milk, 1 teaspoon* at a time, to make an icing of spreading consistency. If desired, tint with *paste food coloring.*

Decorative Frosting: In a medium bowl, combine 4 cups sifted *powdered sugar* and 3 tablespoons *milk*. Stir in enough additional *milk, 1 teaspoon* at a time, to make a frosting of piping consistency. If desired, tint with *paste food coloring.*

Anise Tea Biscuits

Prep: 40 minutes • Bake: 20 minutes per batch

2½ cup cups all-purpose flour
⅓ cup granulated sugar
1½ teaspoons finely shredded orange peel
1 teaspoon anise seed, crushed
1 cup butter
Coarse, colored, and/or pearl sugar

1. In a large bowl, combine flour, granulated sugar, orange peel, and anise seed. Using a pastry blender, cut in butter until mixture resembles fine crumbs. Knead gently until mixture clings together and forms a ball. Divide dough in half.

2. On a lightly floured surface, roll dough, half at a time, to slightly less than ½ inch thickness. Cut with 1½- to 2-inch scalloped or round cookie cutter. On an ungreased cookie sheet, arrange the cutouts 1 inch apart. Sprinkle with coarse sugar.

3. Bake in a 325° oven 20 to 25 minutes or until bottoms just begin to brown. Remove from cookie sheet; cool on wire rack. *Makes 30 to 36 cookies.*

Ginger Tea Biscuits: Prepare and bake Anise Tea Biscuits as directed, except substitute 1 teaspoon grated *fresh ginger* for the anise seed.

Eggnog Cookies

Prep: 45 minutes • Chill: 2 hours • Bake: 10 minutes per batch

2 cups all-purpose flour
1 cup granulated sugar
¾ teaspoon baking powder
¼ teaspoon salt
¼ teaspoon ground nutmeg or ground cardamom
⅔ cup butter
1 slightly beaten egg
¼ cup dairy or canned eggnog
½ cup finely crushed butterscotch- or rum-flavored hard candies (about twenty-five 1-inch candies)
1 recipe Eggnog Icing
Coarse, colored, and/or pearl sugar

1. In a large bowl, stir together flour, granulated sugar, baking powder, salt, and nutmeg. Using a pastry blender, cut in butter until pieces are pea-size. Make a well in center of flour mixture.

2. In a small bowl, combine egg and eggnog; add all at once to flour mixture. Stir until moistened. Cover and refrigerate about 2 hours or until easy to handle.

3. Line a cookie sheet with foil; set aside. On a well-floured surface, roll dough to ¼ inch thickness. Cut with 2½- to 3-inch cookie cutters. On the prepared cookie sheet, arrange cutouts 1 inch apart. Cut small shapes out of cookie centers. Fill each center with candy.

4. Bake in a 375° oven for 10 to 12 minutes or until edges are firm and light brown. Cool on cookie sheet for 5 minutes. Carefully transfer cookies, still on the foil, to a wire rack; cool.

5. Carefully peel foil from bottoms of cookies. Spread tops with Eggnog Icing. Sprinkle with coarse sugar. *Makes 24 to 36 cookies.*

Eggnog Icing: In a medium bowl, stir together 3 cups sifted *powdered sugar* and ¼ teaspoon *rum extract*. Stir in enough *dairy or canned eggnog* (2 to 3 tablespoons) to make an icing of spreading consistency.

Remember—the word "biscuit" is the British term for "cookie." The anise in these cookies is a licorice-flavored spice that the Spanish introduced when they settled in the South and West.

Eggnog Cookies

Golden butterscotch candies create stained-glass centers in these delicate eggnog-flavored cutouts, a contemporary twist on the old-fashioned sugar cookie. To keep the dough from sticking to the cutter, dip the edge of the cutter into flour after every few cuts.

Pecan Balls

Prep: 30 minutes • Bake: 12 minutes per batch

- 1 cup butter
- ½ cup granulated sugar
- ¼ teaspoon salt
- 2 teaspoons vanilla
- 2 cups all-purpose flour
- 1 cup finely chopped pecans
  Extra-fine granulated sugar or sifted powdered sugar

Pecan Balls

1. In a large bowl, beat butter with an electric mixer on medium to high speed for 30 seconds. Add the ½ cup granulated sugar and the salt. Beat until combined. Beat in vanilla. Beat in as much of the flour as you can with the mixer. Using a wooden spoon, stir in any remaining flour. Stir in pecans.

2. Shape slightly rounded teaspoons of the dough into ¾-inch balls. On an ungreased cookie sheet, arrange balls 1 inch apart.

3. Bake in a 350° oven about 12 minutes or just until bottoms begin to brown. While cookies are still warm, roll them in extra-fine granulated sugar or powdered sugar. Place cookies on a wire rack; cool. *Makes about 72 cookies.*

Cornmeal Ribbons

Prep: 30 minutes • Chill: 3 hours • Bake: 7 minutes per batch

- ⅔ cup butter
- ⅔ cup granulated sugar
- 1 teaspoon baking powder
- ¼ teaspoon salt
- 1 egg
- 1½ teaspoons finely shredded lemon peel
- 1 teaspoon vanilla
- ½ cup yellow cornmeal
- 1½ cups all-purpose flour
- 1 recipe Lemon Icing
  Yellow colored sugar (optional)

1. In a large bowl, beat butter with an electric mixer on medium to high spread for 30 seconds. Add granulated sugar, baking powder, and salt. Beat until combined, scraping bowl. Beat in egg, lemon peel, and vanilla until combined. Beat in cornmeal and as much of the flour as you can with the mixer. Using a wooden spoon, stir in any remaining flour. Divide dough in half. Cover and refrigerate about 3 hours or until dough is easy to handle.

2. On a lightly floured surface, roll dough, half at a time, into a 10×8-inch rectangle. Using a fluted pastry wheel, trim edges. Cut rectangle in half lengthwise. Cut crosswise into 1¼-inch-wide strips. On an ungreased cookie sheet, arrange strips 1 inch apart.

3. Bake in a 375° oven for 7 to 8 minutes or until edges are light brown. Remove from cookie sheet; cool on a wire rack. Spread with Lemon Icing and, if desired, sprinkle with colored sugar. *Makes 32 cookies.*

Lemon Icing: In a small bowl, stir together 1½ cups sifted *powdered sugar* and 2 teaspoons *lemon juice.* Stir in enough *milk* (1 to 2 tablespoons) to make an icing of spreading consistency.

Hickory Nut Sandwich Cookies
Prep: 50 minutes • Chill: 3 hours • Bake: 12 minutes per batch

- 1 cup butter
- ¾ cup sugar
- 1½ teaspoons vanilla
- 1¾ cups all-purpose flour
- ¾ cup finely ground hickory nuts, pecans, or black walnuts
- ½ cup finely chopped hickory nuts, pecans, or black walnuts
- 3 ounces bittersweet or semisweet chocolate, chopped
- 1 teaspoon shortening
- 1 recipe Vanilla Buttercream

1. In a large bowl, beat butter with an electric mixer on medium to high speed for 30 seconds. Add sugar and vanilla. Beat until combined, scraping bowl. Beat in as much of the flour as you can with the mixer. Stir in any remaining flour and the ¾ cup ground nuts. Divide dough in half. Shape each half into a 6-inch-long roll. On waxed paper, roll in the ½ cup finely chopped nuts to coat. Wrap each roll in plastic wrap. Refrigerate for at least 3 hours or up to 24 hours.

2. Using a sharp knife, cut dough into slightly less than ¼-inch-thick slices. On an ungreased cookie sheet, arrange slices 1 inch apart.

3. Bake in a 325° oven for 12 to 15 minutes or until bottoms of cookies are light brown. Remove from cookie sheet; cool cookies on a wire rack.

4. In a heavy, small saucepan, heat and stir chocolate and shortening over low heat until melted. Using a small, clean pastry brush, paint bottoms of *half* of the cookies with chocolate. Place cookies, chocolate sides up, on a wire rack. Let chocolate set.

5. To assemble, spread the bottom of each plain cookie with *1 rounded teaspoon* of Vanilla Buttercream. Place a coated cookie, chocolate side down, on frosting. Store in refrigerator. *Makes about 30 cookies.*

Vanilla Buttercream: In a small bowl, beat 2 *egg yolks;* set aside. In a heavy, small saucepan, combine ⅓ cup *sugar* and 2 tablespoons *water.* Bring to boiling; remove from heat. Gradually stir about half of the sugar mixture into egg yolks. Return egg yolk mixture to remaining sugar mixture. Bring to a gentle boil; reduce heat. Cook and stir for 2 minutes. Remove from heat. Stir in ½ teaspoon *vanilla.* Cool to room temperature. In a large bowl beat ½ cup *butter* with an electric mixer on medium to high speed for 30 seconds. Add cooled sugar mixture; beat until combined. If necessary, refrigerate until easy to spread.

If one cookie is good, then two cookies stacked with a rich buttercream filling is surely better. Double-decker cookies that you can twist apart have been an American favorite since the Oreo cookie was invented in 1912. For these nutty cookies, choose from the three native American nuts—hickory nuts, black walnuts, or pecans.

Hickory Nut Sandwich Cookies

Cranberry-Pecan Bars

Cranberry-Pecan Bars

Cranberry-Pecan Bars

Prep: 30 minutes • Bake: 15 minutes + 25 minutes

    1   cup all-purpose flour
    2   tablespoons sugar
    ½   cup butter
    ½   cup finely chopped pecans
    1   cup sugar
    2   tablespoons all-purpose flour
    2   beaten eggs
    2   tablespoons milk
    1   tablespoon finely shredded orange peel
    1   teaspoon vanilla
    1   cup chopped fresh cranberries
    ½   cup coconut
    ½   cup finely chopped pecans

1. For crust, in a medium bowl, stir together the 1 cup flour and the 2 tablespoons sugar. Using a pastry blender, cut in butter until mixture resembles coarse crumbs. Stir in

½ cup pecans. Press evenly onto the bottom of an ungreased 13×9×2-inch baking pan. Bake in a 350° oven for 15 minutes.

2. Meanwhile, in a large bowl, stir together the 1 cup sugar and the 2 tablespoons flour. Stir in eggs, milk, orange peel, and vanilla until combined. Stir in cranberries, coconut, and ½ cup pecans. Spread onto crust.

3. Bake for 25 to 30 minutes or until top is light brown. Place pan on a wire rack. While cookies are still warm, cut into bars. Cool in pan on wire rack. _Makes 36 bars._

Pumpkin Cheesecake Bars

Prep: 30 minutes • Bake: 10 minutes + 25 minutes • Chill: 4 hours

    2   cups finely crushed gingersnaps (about
            30 cookies)
    ¼   cup butter, melted
    ⅓   cup canned pumpkin
    1   tablespoon all-purpose flour
    1   teaspoon pumpkin pie spice
    3   8-ounce packages cream cheese, softened
    1   cup sugar
    1½ teaspoons vanilla
    3   eggs

1. For crust, in a medium bowl, stir together gingersnaps and melted butter. Lightly grease a 13×9×2-inch baking pan; press crumb mixture evenly onto bottom. Bake in a 325° oven about 10 minutes or until crust is firm. Cool in pan on a wire rack.

2. Meanwhile, for pumpkin batter, in a small bowl stir together pumpkin, flour, and pumpkin pie spice; set aside.

3. For cream cheese batter, in a large bowl, beat cream cheese with an electric mixer on low to medium speed until smooth. Add sugar and vanilla. Beat until combined, scraping bowl. Add eggs, one at a time, beating on low speed after each addition just until combined.

4. Stir about _one-third_ of the cream cheese batter into the pumpkin batter until smooth. Pour remaining cream cheese batter over crust. Place large spoonfuls of pumpkin batter randomly over cream cheese batter. Using the tip of a table knife or a thin metal spatula, gently swirl the two batters together. Bake in the 325° oven for 25 to 30 minutes or just until center is set.

5. Cool thoroughly in pan on a wire rack. Cover and refrigerate at least 4 hours before cutting into bars. Store in the refrigerator. _Makes 24 bars._

Double Citrus-Hazelnut Bars
Prep: 30 minutes • Bake: 10 minutes + 20 minutes

⅓ cup butter
¼ cup granulated sugar
1 cup all-purpose flour
⅓ cup finely chopped toasted hazelnuts
     (filberts) or chopped almonds
2 eggs
¾ cup granulated sugar
2 tablespoons all-purpose flour
1 teaspoon finely shredded orange peel
2 tablespoons orange juice
1 teaspoon finely shredded lemon peel
1 tablespoon lemon juice
½ teaspoon baking powder
   Powdered sugar (optional)

1. For crust, in a medium bowl, beat butter with an electric mixer on medium to high speed for 30 seconds. Add the ¼ cup granulated sugar. Beat until combined, scraping bowl. Beat in the 1 cup flour and about *half* of the nuts until mixture is crumbly. Press nut mixture evenly onto the bottom of an ungreased 8×8×2-inch baking pan. Bake in a 350° oven about 10 minutes or until light brown.

2. Meanwhile, in a small bowl, stir together eggs, the ¾ cup granulated sugar, the 2 tablespoons flour, the orange peel, orange juice, lemon peel, lemon juice, and baking powder. Beat on medium speed for 2 minutes. Pour over crust. Sprinkle with remaining nuts.

3. Bake in the 350° oven about 20 minutes or until edges are light brown and center is set. Cool in pan on a wire rack. If desired, sift powdered sugar over top. Cut into bars. Store in the refrigerator. *Makes 20 bars.*

Double Citrus-Hazelnut Bars

D elightfully light and tangy lemon bars grace many a tea table at holiday time. This citrus variation simply adds orange and hazelnuts to the recipe that Grandma made every Christmas.

Rum and Eggnog Cakes (recipe, page 123)
Cranberry Syrup (recipe, page 114)

Gifts from the Heart

The American tradition of exchanging gifts at Christmas seems to have originated with Saint Nicholas bringing oranges, candy, and cookies to the Dutch children in New Amsterdam and New York City. Saint Nicholas would be glad to know that humble food gifts are as popular today as they were in the 1700s. And fortunately, we still think that the best gifts are homemade, for they embrace the priceless presents of time and thought. Thankfully, we no longer have to grow what we give, nor toil over a wood-burning stove. All we need are a few hours and some time-tested recipes, such as the American heritage ideas in this chapter, to make delicious memories for our loved ones.

Stock up on cranberries at Thanksgiving so you can make batches of this sparkling ruby-red syrup for holiday gifts. (The berries freeze well, letting you stir up this syrup and any of the book's recipes that call for fresh cranberries anytime.) On your gift tag, suggest serving the syrup with pancakes, waffles, and even ice cream. If you like, you also can tuck in the recipes for Apple Griddle Cakes (recipe, page 52) and Pumpkin Waffles (recipe, page 53). The syrup is also pictured on page 112.

Cranberry Syrup

Cranberry Syrup
Prep: 15 minutes • Cook: 30 minutes

2½ cups cranberry juice
  1 cup fresh cranberries
¾ cup light-colored corn syrup
¼ cup sugar

1. In a medium saucepan, combine cranberry juice, cranberries, corn syrup, and sugar. Cook and stir until sugar is dissolved. Bring to a rolling boil over medium-high heat; reduce heat to medium. Boil, uncovered, for 30 to 40 minutes or until liquid is reduced to 2½ cups.

2. Line a colander with 100%-cotton cheesecloth or coffee filters. Pour syrup through the colander and let it drain into a bowl. Discard cranberries.

3. Transfer strained syrup to half-pint bottles or jars. Store syrup, covered, in the refrigerator for up to 2 weeks. *Makes 2 cups syrup.*

Herb Vinegar

Prep: 15 minutes • Stand: 2 weeks

½ cup tightly packed fresh tarragon, thyme,
    mint, rosemary, or basil leaves
2 cups white wine vinegar
    Fresh herb sprig (optional)

1. Wash herb and pat dry with paper towels. In a small stainless-steel or enamel saucepan, combine herb and vinegar. Bring almost to boiling. Remove from heat; cover with 100%-cotton cheesecloth; cool.

2. Pour mixture into a 1-quart jar. Cover with a nonmetallic lid (or plastic wrap and metal lid); tightly seal. Let stand in a cool, dark place for 2 weeks.

3. Line a colander with several layers of 100%-cotton cheesecloth or coffee filters. Pour vinegar mixture through the colander and let drain into a bowl. Discard herbs.

4. Transfer strained vinegar to half-pint jars or bottles. If desired, add a sprig of fresh herb to each jar. Cover jars with nonmetallic lids (or plastic wrap and metal lids); tightly seal. Store vinegar in a cool, dark place for up to 6 months. *Makes about 2 cups vinegar.*

This versatile vinegar stores for up to six months. You can multiply the recipe to make several gifts. If you like, tuck in the recipes for Beet and Apple Salad (recipe, page 14) or Fig and Orange Salad (recipe, page 12).

Fruit Cordial

Prep: 30 minutes • Stand: 1 week

1½ cups sugar
2 large mangoes, 2 medium oranges, or
    6 medium pears
1 750-milliliter bottle vodka (3½ cups)

1. In a small saucepan, heat together sugar and 1 cup *water,* stirring until sugar is dissolved. Remove from heat; cool.

2. If using mangoes, peel, pit, and chop fruit. If using oranges, remove thin orange layer of peel with a sharp knife, avoiding the bitter white layer. Use peel to prepare cordial (reserve fruit for another use). If using pears, peel, core, and thinly slice fruit.

3. Pour cooled sugar mixture into a 2-quart jar. Add vodka and mangoes, orange peel, or pears; stir gently. Cover jar tightly. Let stand in a cool place for at least 1 week or up to 2 weeks for mango cordial or up to 3 weeks for orange or pear cordial.

4. Line a colander with several layers of 100%-cotton cheesecloth or coffee filters. Pour fruit mixture through the colander and let it drain into a large bowl. Discard fruit.

5. Transfer strained cordial to half-pint bottles or jars. Store, covered, at room temperature for up to 2 weeks. *Makes 5 cups cordial.*

Mango Cordial

Sipping a glass of cordial is a Christmas custom that dates back to the holiday open houses of the 1800s. Revive the tradition this year by giving small decanters of after-dinner spirits to those near and dear to you. Tie a festive garland around each bottle.

Corn Relish

Prep: 1½ hours • Process: 15 minutes

This festive relish has roots in the farmlands of the Pennsylvania Dutch and Shaker communities. Both groups prided themselves on their canned products. Find some holiday-themed jar tops, or put a little fabric and batting between the lid and screw-top. On your gift card, suggest serving the relish with grilled burgers and meats.

16 to 18 fresh ears of corn
2 cups water
3 cups chopped celery (6 stalks)
1½ cups chopped red sweet peppers
1½ cups chopped green sweet peppers
1 cup chopped onions (2 medium)
3 cups vinegar
2 cups sugar
4 teaspoons dry mustard
2 teaspoons pickling salt
2 teaspoons celery seed
1 teaspoon ground turmeric
3 tablespoons cornstarch
2 tablespoons cold water

1. Cut corn from cobs (do not scrape cobs). Measure 8 cups corn. In an 8- to 10-quart stainless-steel, enamel, or nonstick heavy kettle, combine corn and the 2 cups water. Bring to boiling; reduce heat. Cover and simmer for 4 to 5 minutes or until corn is nearly tender; drain.

2. In the same kettle, combine corn, celery, sweet peppers, and onions. Stir in vinegar, sugar, mustard, pickling salt, celery seed, and turmeric. Bring to boiling; reduce heat. Simmer, uncovered, for 5 minutes, stirring occasionally.

3. In a small bowl, combine cornstarch and the 2 tablespoons cold water; add to corn mixture. Cook and stir until thickened and bubbly; cook and stir for 2 minutes more.

4. Ladle hot relish into hot, sterilized 1-pint canning jars, leaving a ½-inch headspace (see Canning Basics, page 119). Wipe jar rims and adjust lids. Process in a boiling-water canner for 15 minutes (start timing when water returns to boil). Remove jars and cool on wire racks. *Makes 7 pints.*

Sweet Cucumber Pickles

Prep: 40 minutes • Chill: 3 hours • Process: 10 minutes

The familiar Mason jar only has been around since 1858, when it was invented by American John Mason. The tight-sealing jar made home canning much easier and safer for people who wanted to share the fruits of their gardens with family and friends. Suggest serving these crunchy slices with cold meats, burgers, and sandwiches.

4 quarts (16 cups) sliced medium cucumbers
8 medium white onions, sliced
⅓ cup pickling salt
3 cloves garlic, halved
Cracked ice
4 cups sugar
3 cups cider vinegar
2 tablespoons mustard seed
1½ teaspoons ground turmeric
1½ teaspoons celery seed

1. In a 6- to 8-quart stainless-steel, enamel, or nonstick kettle, combine cucumbers, onions, pickling salt, and garlic. Add 2 inches of cracked ice. Cover with lid and refrigerate for at least 3 hours or up to 12 hours.

2. Remove any remaining ice. Drain mixture well in a large colander. Remove garlic.

3. In the same kettle, combine sugar, vinegar, mustard seed, turmeric, and celery seed. Bring to boiling. Add drained cucumber mixture. Return to boiling.

4. Ladle hot cucumber mixture and liquid into hot, sterilized 1-pint canning jars, leaving a ½-inch headspace (see Canning Basics, page 119). Wipe jar rims and adjust lids. Process in a boiling-water canner for 10 minutes (start timing when water returns to boil). Remove jars and cool on wire racks. *Makes 7 pints.*

Rum Fruit Topping

Rum Fruit Topping
Prep: 30 minutes • Chill: 3 days

1½ cups packed brown sugar
1 cup water
4 large pears, cored and cut up
4 medium nectarines or peeled peaches, pitted
   and sliced, or one 16-ounce package
   frozen unsweetened peach slices, thawed
2 cups seedless red grapes, halved (optional)
1 medium pineapple, peeled, cored, and cut up
2½ to 3 cups rum

1. For syrup, in a small saucepan, combine brown sugar and water. Cook and stir over medium-low heat until sugar is dissolved. Remove from heat; cool.

2. In a large nonmetallic bowl, combine fruit; pour in syrup. Ladle fruit and syrup into 1-pint jars. Add enough of the rum to cover the fruit; stir gently to combine. Cover and refrigerate for at least 3 days before serving or giving away. Store, covered, in the refrigerator for up to 4 months, stirring occasionally (the top layer of fruit may darken during storage). Use portions as desired; replenish fruit as needed. *Makes about 12 cups.*

To replenish fruit topping: Add 2 cups chopped *fruit* and ½ cup packed *brown sugar* to replace every 2 cups of fruit and syrup used. Store in the refrigerator for several days before using again.

Here's a gift that keeps on giving. Also known as friendship fruit, this topping is based on a German and Austrian specialty known as "rumtopf," which means "rum pot." Once made, portions are shared with friends, who start their own topper, which they in turn share with other friends. To decorate the jars as pictured, purchase silk rope and artificial fruits and leaves at your local crafts shop. On your gift card, suggest serving the topping warm over pound cake, gingerbread, or ice cream—and remember to include the directions for replenishing the topping.

Tangerine Marmalade

Tangerine Marmalade
Prep: 30 minutes • Process: 5 minutes • Cool: 4 hours

10 to 12 medium tangerines
 7 cups sugar
½ of a 6-ounce package (1 pouch) liquid
    fruit pectin

1. Peel tangerines, reserving peel. Section
fruit over a bowl to catch juice; discard
membrane from sections. Chop fruit,
removing seeds (you should have 3 cups
fruit and ¾ cup juice). Scrape excess white
from peel. Cut enough of the peel into very
thin strips to measure ¾ cup.

2. In an 8- to 10-quart Dutch oven or kettle,
combine chopped fruit, juice, strips of peel,
and sugar. Bring to a full rolling boil.
Quickly stir in pectin; return to a full boil.
Boil for 1 minute, stirring constantly.
Remove from heat. Using a metal spoon,
quickly skim off foam.

3. Ladle hot mixture into hot, sterilized half-
pint or 4-ounce canning jars, leaving a
½-inch headspace (see Canning Basics at
right). Wipe jar rims and adjust lids. Process
in a boiling-water canner for 5 minutes (start
timing when water returns to boil).

4. Remove jars and cool on wire racks for
2 hours. Turn jars upside down; cool for
2 hours more. Turn jars right sides up.
Marmalade may need up to 2 weeks to set.
Makes 7 half-pints or fourteen 4-ounce jars.

Double Lemon Curd

Start to finish: 20 minutes

   1 cup sugar
1½ teaspoons cornstarch
   4 teaspoons finely shredded lemon peel
         (set aside)
⅓ cup lemon juice
¼ cup butter, cut up
   3 beaten eggs

1. In a medium saucepan (do not use aluminum), combine sugar and cornstarch. Stir in lemon juice; add butter. Cook and stir over medium heat until thickened and bubbly. Cook and stir for 2 minutes more.

2. Stir about *half* of the hot mixture into eggs. Return mixture to saucepan. Reduce heat; cook and stir for 1 to 2 minutes or until mixture begins to thicken. Do not boil.

3. Pour lemon curd through a small mesh strainer and let it drain into a bowl; discard any egg particles. Gently stir lemon peel into hot mixture and pour into 4-ounce jars. Cool. Store, covered, in the refrigerator for up to 1 month. *Makes 1¾ cups.*

The British brought tangy-sweet lemon curd to our tea and coffee tables. It's scrumptious slathered on toast, so package it with English muffins or crumpets. Or use it as a cake or tart filling. For tarts, purchase miniature tart phyllo shells.

Apple Butter

Prep: 1 hour • Cook: 2 hours • Process: 5 minutes

4½ pounds tart cooking apples, cored and
         quartered (about 14 medium)
   3 cups apple juice or apple cider
   2 cups sugar
1½ teaspoons ground cinnamon
½ teaspoon ground cloves
½ teaspoon ground allspice

1. In a heavy, 8- to 10-quart kettle, combine apples and apple juice. Bring to boiling; reduce heat. Cover and simmer for 30 minutes, stirring occasionally.

2. Press through a food mill or sieve until you have 8½ cups. Return to kettle. Stir in sugar, cinnamon, cloves, and allspice. Bring to boiling; reduce heat. Cook, uncovered, over very low heat about 1½ hours or until mixture is very thick and mounds on a spoon, stirring often.

3. Ladle hot apple butter into hot, sterilized half-pint canning jars, leaving a ¼-inch headspace (see Canning Basics below). Wipe jar rims and adjust lids. Process in a boiling-water canner for 5 minutes (start timing when water returns to boil). Remove jars and cool on wire racks. *Makes 8 half-pints.*

Apples and other fruits have been traditional stocking stuffers for centuries. This year, instead of fresh apples, tuck in jars of this appealing fruit-and-spice spread. Or pair a jar of apple butter with a loaf of Anadama or Sally Lunn Bread (recipes, page 63.)

Canning Basics

• Use only standard canning jars. To prepare jars, wash them in hot, soapy water; rinse thoroughly. To sterilize jars, immerse them in boiling water for 10 minutes. Prepare screw bands and new flat metal lids with a built-in sealing compound according to manufacturer's directions.
• Fill canner half full of water; cover and heat over high heat until boiling. Heat additional water in another kettle.
• When the water is hot, fill each jar and place it on rack in canner. After the last jar

has been added, add enough additional boiling water to put tops of jars 1 inch below the water line. Cover; heat to a brisk, rolling boil. Now begin the processing timing. Keep water boiling gently during processing.
• When jars are completely cool (12 to 24 hours), press the center of each lid to check the seal. If dip in lid holds, the jar is sealed. If lid bounces up and down, the jar isn't sealed. (The contents of unsealed jars can be refrigerated and used within 2 to 3 days.)

To prevent spoilage, homemade relishes, pickles, and jam products need to be processed in a boiling-water canner (a large kettle with a lid and rack designed to hold canning jars). The tips at left will assure that you make top-quality home-canned products.

This layered cookie mix lets your lucky friends indulge in fresh-from-the-oven cookies whenever they want. To make four jars, stir together four times the amount of flour, spices, and shortening. Next time, vary the mix by substituting ⅔ cup semisweet chocolate and/or white baking pieces for the cherries and raisins. Remember to attach the directions for baking the cookies.

Hearty vegetable soups have fortified many a family over the years. Here's a dry-mix version you can give for savoring on the cold winter days ahead. For fun, package it in a soup bowl or mug, sealed tightly in plastic wrap, with the cooking directions, of course.

Cookies-in-a-Jar

Prep: 15 minutes

- ¾ cup all-purpose flour
- ½ teaspoon baking powder
- ⅛ teaspoon baking soda
- ⅛ teaspoon salt
- ½ cup shortening that does not require refrigeration
- ½ cup packed brown sugar
- ⅓ cup dried tart red cherries
- ⅓ cup golden raisins
- 1 cup rolled oats
- ¼ cup chopped pecans or walnuts
- ¼ cup flaked coconut

1. In a small bowl, stir together flour, baking powder, baking soda, and salt. Using a pastry blender, cut in shortening until mixture resembles coarse crumbs.

2. In a 1-quart glass jar, layer flour mixture, brown sugar, cherries, raisins, oats, pecans, and coconut. Tap jar gently on the counter to settle each layer before adding the next one. Store, covered, in the refrigerator for up to 6 weeks.

Cookies-in-a-Jar

To Prepare Cookies: In a large bowl, stir mix until combined. Stir in 1 *egg* and 1 teaspoon *vanilla* until mixed. Drop dough by rounded teaspoons 2 inches apart onto an ungreased cookie sheet. Bake in a 375° oven for 8 to 10 minutes or until edges are light brown. Remove from cookie sheet; cool on a wire rack. *Makes about 24 cookies.*

Lentil Stew Mix

Prep: 5 minutes

- 1¼ cups green or brown lentils
- ¼ cup dried minced onion
- ¼ cup dried green sweet pepper
- 1 teaspoon salt
- 1 teaspoon dried thyme, crushed
- ½ teaspoon fennel seed, crushed
- ¼ teaspoon crushed red pepper

In a medium bowl, combine lentils, onion, green pepper, salt, thyme, fennel seed, and crushed red pepper. Transfer to an airtight container. Store, covered, in a cool, dry place for up to 1 year.

To Prepare Stew: In a large saucepan, bring 6 cups *water* to boiling. Stir in dry mix; reduce heat. Cover and simmer for 35 to 40 minutes or until lentils are soft. *Makes 4 servings.*

Blueberry Scone Mix
Prep: 15 minutes

- ⅓ cup Vanilla Sugar
- 2 cups all-purpose flour
- ¼ cup nonfat dry milk powder
- 2 teaspoons baking powder
- 1 teaspoon dried lemon peel
- ¼ teaspoon salt
- ⅓ cup shortening that does not require refrigeration
- 1 cup dried blueberries

1. In a large bowl, stir together Vanilla Sugar, flour, dry milk powder, baking powder, lemon peel, and salt. Using a pastry blender, cut in shortening until mixture resembles coarse crumbs.

2. In a 1-quart glass jar, layer flour mixture and blueberries. Tap jar gently on the counter to settle contents. If necessary, add additional blueberries to fill small gaps. Store, covered, in the refrigerator for up to 6 weeks or in the freezer for up to 6 months.

Minty Hot Cocoa Mix
Prep: 10 minutes

- ⅔ cup sugar
- ½ cup unsweetened cocoa powder
- 1⅓ cups nonfat dry milk powder
- 1 10-ounce package (1⅔ cups) mint-flavored semisweet chocolate pieces
- Miniature marshmallows (optional)
- Candy canes (optional)

1. In two 1-pint glass milk bottles or jars, layer sugar, cocoa powder, dry milk powder, and chocolate pieces, dividing ingredients equally. Tap bottles or jars gently on the counter to settle each layer before adding the next one. If necessary, add additional chocolate pieces to fill small gaps. Store, covered, in a cool, dry place for up to 6 weeks.

Vanilla Sugar: Fill a 1-quart jar with 4 cups *sugar*. Cut a *vanilla bean* in half lengthwise and insert both halves into sugar. Store, covered, in a cool, dry place for several weeks before using, then store until needed. *Makes 4 cups.*

To Prepare Scones: In a large bowl, stir mix until combined. Add 1 beaten *egg* and ¼ cup *water;* stir just until moistened. Turn dough out onto a lightly floured surface. Quickly knead dough by gently folding and pressing for 12 to 15 strokes or until nearly smooth. Pat dough into an 8-inch circle. Cut into 10 wedges. On an ungreased baking sheet, arrange wedges 1 inch apart. If desired, brush with *milk* and sprinkle with *coarse sugar.* Bake in a 400° oven for 12 to 15 minutes or until golden. Remove from baking sheet; cool slightly on a wire rack. Serve warm. *Makes 10 scones.*

Minty Hot Cocoa Mix

To Prepare Cocoa: In a large saucepan, stir the contents of 1 bottle of mix until combined. Stir in 2½ cups *water.* Cook and stir over medium heat until chocolate is melted and mixture is heated through. Pour into 4 mugs. If desired, serve with tiny marshmallows and candy canes. *Makes 4 servings per bottle of mix.*

*T*riple this recipe to create three gifts for scone-loving friends. To drum up a Scottish look, tie your gift with a plaid ribbon or plaid-covered jar top. Include an assortment of teas with your package.

*G*randma would chase away winter chills with mugs of hot cocoa. Now everyone on your Christmas list can do the same with this hot cocoa mix. Line up the ingredients in an assembly line to make several mixes. If you can't find milk bottles, use any pretty pint bottles or jars, and include candy canes to use as stirring sticks.

Gingerbread Loaves

Gingerbread Loaves
Prep: 25 minutes • Bake: 25 minutes

1½ cups all-purpose flour
 1 teaspoon baking powder
 1 teaspoon ground cinnamon
 ½ teaspoon ground ginger
 ¼ teaspoon baking soda
 ¼ teaspoon salt
 1 egg
 ⅓ cup light-colored molasses
 ⅓ cup cooking oil
 ¼ cup packed brown sugar
 ¼ cup milk
 1 recipe Lemon Glaze
   Chopped crystallized ginger (optional)
   Lemon slice twists (optional)

1. Grease the bottoms and halfway up the sides of two 5¾×3×2-inch individual loaf pans; set aside.

2. In a medium bowl, stir together flour, baking powder, cinnamon, ginger, baking soda, and salt. Make a well in the center of flour mixture; set aside.

3. In another medium bowl, combine egg, molasses, oil, brown sugar, and milk. Add egg mixture all at once to flour mixture. Stir just until moistened (batter should be lumpy). Spoon into the prepared pans.

4. Bake in a 350° oven for 25 to 30 minutes or until a wooden toothpick inserted near centers comes out clean. Cool in pans on wire racks for 10 minutes. Remove from pans. Cool on wire racks. Wrap tightly. Store in the refrigerator for up to 3 days or in the freezer for up to 3 months.

5. Before giving, drizzle loaves with Lemon Glaze. If desired, decorate with crystallized ginger and lemon twists. *Makes 2 loaves.*

Lemon Glaze: In a small bowl, stir together 1 cup sifted *powdered sugar* and 1 teaspoon *lemon juice or vanilla.* Stir in enough *milk, 1 teaspoon* at a time, to make a glaze of drizzling consistency.

Rum and Eggnog Cakes
Prep: 40 minutes • Bake: 30 minutes • Store: 1 day

2¼ cups all-purpose flour
  2 teaspoons baking powder
  ¾ teaspoon ground nutmeg
  1 cup diced mixed candied fruits and peels
  ½ cup golden raisins
  ½ cup chopped pecans
  2 tablespoons all-purpose flour
1½ cups butter
  1 cup sugar
  3 eggs
1¼ cups regular or reduced-fat dairy eggnog
  ¾ to 1¼ cups rum or ¾ to 1¼ cups orange
        juice plus ½ teaspoon rum extract
  1 recipe Eggnog Glaze
    Sliced candied cherries (optional)

1. Grease and lightly flour twelve 4-inch individual fluted tube pans or one 10-inch fluted tube pan; set aside.

2. In a medium bowl, stir together the 2¼ cups flour, the baking powder, and nutmeg; set aside. In a small bowl, toss together candied fruits, raisins, pecans, and the 2 tablespoons flour; set aside.

3. In a large bowl, beat butter with an electric mixer on medium to high speed for 30 seconds. Gradually add sugar, beating until light and fluffy. Add eggs, *one* at a time, beating for 1 minute after each.

4. Add flour mixture and eggnog alternately to butter mixture, beating on low speed after each addition just until combined. (Do not overbeat.) Stir in *¼ cup* of the rum or orange juice mixture. Fold in fruit mixture. Pour batter into prepared pans.

5. Bake in a 350° oven about 30 minutes for 4-inch pans (55 to 60 minutes for 10-inch pan) or until a wooden toothpick inserted near centers comes out clean. Cool in pans on wire racks for 15 minutes. Remove from pans; cool on wire racks.

6. With a toothpick, poke holes in cakes. Soak 100%-cotton cheesecloth in rum or orange juice mixture, using *1 cup* of the mixture for 4-inch cakes or *½ cup* of the mixture for 10-inch cake. Wrap cakes in moistened cheesecloth. Place in self-sealing plastic bags.

7. Store in the refrigerator for up to 2 days to mellow flavors, drizzling with *¼ cup* of the rum or juice mixture after 1 day.

8. Before giving, drizzle cakes with Eggnog Glaze; let dry. If desired, decorate with candied cherries. *Makes 24 to 30 servings.*

Eggnog Glaze: In a small bowl, stir together 1 cup sifted *powdered sugar*, 1 tablespoon *regular or reduced-fat dairy eggnog*, 1 tablespoon *light-colored corn syrup*, and ½ teaspoon *light rum* or ¼ teaspoon *rum extract*. Stir in enough additional *eggnog*, *1 teaspoon* at a time, to make a glaze of drizzling consistency.

Make-Ahead Tip: Prepare, bake, and cool Rum and Eggnog Cakes as directed, except do not drizzle with rum or juice mixture or drizzle with Eggnog Glaze. Place in freezer bags and freeze for up to 3 months. Thaw in refrigerator. Drizzle with ¼ cup *rum or orange juice*. Before giving, drizzle cakes with Eggnog Glaze; let dry. If desired, decorate with candied cherries.

Toasting the holidays isn't the only way to enjoy eggnog. You can savor it in these elegant miniature cakes. As a token of the season, package the mini cakes on pretty plates you've picked up at a garage sale. Since these cakes keep well, freeze some to serve drop-in guests too. The cakes are also pictured on page 112.

Rum and Eggnog Cakes

Caramel-Nut Corn

Popcorn has been part of our holidays since the Indians taught us to heat dried corn kernels over a fire. We loved to eat it, but we learned to decorate with it too. Strung together, popped kernels made snowy white garlands for our Christmas trees. And, somewhere along the way, came caramel corn, sold with a prize inside. Just for fun, include a surprise trinket when you bag up batches of this crunchy mix.

Caramel-Nut Corn
Prep: 25 minutes • Bake: 20 minutes

Nonstick cooking spray
12 cups popped popcorn (½ to ⅔ cup unpopped)
1½ cups mixed salted nuts
1 cup packed brown sugar
¾ cup butter
½ cup dark-colored corn syrup
½ teaspoon sifted baking soda

1. Lightly coat a roasting pan with nonstick cooking spray. Remove unpopped kernels from popped popcorn. Combine popcorn and nuts in the prepared pan; keep warm in a 300° oven.

2. In a 2-quart saucepan, combine brown sugar, butter, and corn syrup. Bring to boiling over medium heat, stirring constantly (about 12 minutes). Cook and stir for 5 minutes more. Remove from heat. Stir in baking soda (the mixture will foam).

3. Pour caramel mixture over popcorn mixture; stir gently to coat. Bake in the 300° oven for 15 minutes. Stir popcorn mixture. Bake for 5 minutes more.

4. Immediately turn out onto a large piece of foil; cool. Break apart. Store in an airtight container at room temperature for up to 1 week. *Makes about 15 cups.*

124

Orange Breakfast Granola

Prep: 15 minutes • Bake: 30 minutes

- 3 cups regular rolled oats
- ½ cup toasted wheat germ
- ½ cup coarsely chopped hazelnuts (filberts) or sliced almonds
- ⅓ cup honey
- ½ teaspoon finely shredded orange peel
- ⅓ cup orange juice
- ½ teaspoon ground cinnamon
  Nonstick cooking spray
- 1 cup flaked or shredded coconut

1. In a large bowl, stir together the oats, wheat germ, and hazelnuts; set aside.

2. In a small saucepan, stir together honey, orange peel, orange juice, and cinnamon. Bring just to boiling. Pour honey mixture over oat mixture; toss gently to coat.

3. Lightly coat a 15×10×1-inch baking pan with nonstick cooking spray. Spread oat mixture evenly in prepared pan.

4. Bake in a 325° oven for 15 minutes. Stir coconut into oat mixture. Bake for 15 to 20 minutes more or until light brown, stirring once.

5. Immediately turn out onto a large piece of foil; cool. Break apart. Store in an airtight container at room temperature for up to 2 weeks or in the freezer for up to 3 months. *Makes about 5 cups.*

Granola is a relative newcomer to our holiday breakfast tables. In our quest to return to all things natural in the 1970s, it filled our breakfast bowls. Package this homemade health-food favorite in recycled bags or boxes, tie with undyed twine, and decorate with pinecones. Suggest serving it as a breakfast cereal, a trail snack mix, or a topping for ice cream or yogurt.

Key Lime-Macadamia Fudge

Prep: 15 minutes • Chill: 2 hours

- 3 cups white baking pieces
- 1 14-ounce can (1¼ cups) sweetened condensed milk
- 2 teaspoons finely shredded lime peel
- 2 tablespoons bottled Key lime juice or regular lime juice
- 1 cup chopped macadamia nuts, toasted if desired

1. Line an 8×8×2- or 9×9×2-inch baking pan with foil, extending foil over edges of pan. Butter foil; set pan aside.

2. In a heavy, large saucepan, cook and stir baking pieces and sweetened condensed milk over low heat just until baking pieces are melted and mixture is smooth. Remove from heat. Stir in lime peel and lime juice. Stir in macadamia nuts.

3. Spread mixture evenly in the prepared pan. If desired, sprinkle with additional coarsely chopped macadamia nuts. Cover and refrigerate about 2 hours or until firm.

4. Use foil to lift fudge out of pan. Cut fudge into squares. Store in an airtight container at room temperature for up to 1 week or in the freezer for up to 2 months. *Makes 2½ pounds.*

Key Lime-Macadamia Fudge

If you think Christmas just isn't Christmas without homemade fudge, you'll love this tropical white version. It blends sassy Florida Key lime juice with white baking pieces and irresistible macadamia nuts.

Blue Cheese-Walnut Bites

*W*ant the perfect hostess gift? How about something to unwrap and set right out on the buffet table? No need to package cheese with this gift. These easy-to-make nibbles offer blue cheese flavor and cracker crunch all in one bite.

Blue Cheese-Walnut Bites

Prep: 20 minutes • Chill: 2 hours • Bake: 8 minutes per batch

1½ cups all-purpose flour
 2 to 3 teaspoons cracked black pepper
 8 ounces blue cheese
¼ cup butter
 1 cup chopped walnuts
 2 slightly beaten egg yolks

1. In a medium bowl, stir together flour and pepper. Using a pastry blender, cut in cheese and butter until mixture resembles coarse crumbs. Stir in walnuts and egg yolks. Form mixture into a ball; knead until combined.

2. Shape dough into two 9-inch-long logs. If desired, flatten sides of logs, making square logs. Wrap each log in plastic wrap. Refrigerate at least 2 hours.

3. Using a sharp knife, cut logs into ¼-inch-thick slices. On an ungreased baking sheet, arrange slices 1 inch apart.

4. Bake in a 425° oven for 8 to 10 minutes or until bottoms and edges are golden brown. Remove from baking sheet; cool on a wire rack. Serve warm or at room temperature. Store in an airtight container in the refrigerator for up to 1 week. *Makes about 72.*

Trail Mix Bars-in-a-Jar
Prep: 10 minutes

1¼ cups quick-cooking rolled oats
⅓ cup coarsely chopped walnuts or pecans
⅔ cup packed brown sugar
¼ teaspoon ground cinnamon
½ cup semisweet chocolate pieces
½ cup packaged biscuit mix
⅓ cup dried cherries or raisins
¼ cup shelled sunflower seed

In a 1-quart glass jar or canister, layer oats, nuts, brown sugar, cinnamon, chocolate pieces, biscuit mix, cherries, and sunflower seed. Tap jar gently on the counter to settle each layer before adding the next one. Store, covered, at room temperature for up to 1 month.

To Prepare Bars: Grease an 8×8×2-inch baking pan; set aside. In a large bowl, stir mix to combine. Using a wooden spoon, stir in 1 *egg*, 2 tablespoons *milk*, 2 tablespoons *cooking oil*, and 1 teaspoon *vanilla* until combined. Spread in prepared pan. Bake in a 375° oven about 25 minutes or until edges are brown. Cool in pan on a wire rack. Cut into bars. *Makes 16 bars.*

Sweet Sesame Wafers
Prep: 25 minutes • Bake: 10 minutes per batch

¾ cup sesame seed
½ cup butter
2 cups packed brown sugar
½ teaspoon baking powder
¼ teaspoon salt
1 egg
1 teaspoon vanilla
1 cup all-purpose flour

1. Spread the sesame seed in a large shallow baking pan. Toast in a 325° oven about 10 minutes or until golden brown, stirring occasionally. Set aside to cool.

2. Meanwhile, in a medium bowl, beat butter with an electric mixer on medium to high speed for 30 seconds. Add brown sugar, baking powder, and salt. Beat until combined, scraping bowl. Beat in egg and vanilla until combined. Beat in flour on low speed just until combined. Stir in the cooled sesame seed.

3. Line a cookie sheet with foil. Butter the foil. Shape level teaspoons of the dough into balls. On the prepared cookie sheet, arrange balls 2 inches apart (cookies will spread as they bake).

4. Bake in the 325° oven for 10 to 12 minutes or until golden brown. Cool on the cookie sheet for 1 minute. Remove from cookie sheet; cool on a wire rack. Store in an airtight container at room temperature for up to 3 days or in the freezer for up to 3 months. *Makes about 96 cookies.*

It's doubtful that the cowboys and wagon masters had such delicious snacks on the trail, but there's no reason your hikers and bikers should go hungry. This mix—chockful of nuts, fruits, and chocolate—bakes up into chewy bars that are perfect for a take-along snack. It makes a great gift for the winter sports enthusiasts on your list.

African-American cooks have been making sesame seed (benne) cookies for hundreds of years. In fact, legend says eating the nutty seeds brings good luck and good health. If the superstition is true, pass good fortune along to everyone in your crowd by handing out small gift bags of these crisp, toffee-like morsels.

Gingerbread Log Cabin

Gingerbread houses are the stuff that fairy tales are made of, for it was the Grimm brothers who popularized the witch's gingerbread house in their story *Hansel and Gretel*. German cooks elaborated on the theme here in the United States, molding their sturdy gingerbread or *lebkuchen* dough into all sorts of American-style buildings. We've taken a little license by constructing a fanciful log cabin in the woods, like the pioneers on the frontier would have built. With the directions on the following pages, you can build one with your children this year.

Gingerbread Log Cabin
(recipe, page 130)

Gingerbread Log Cabin

Pattern pieces:

1 floor: 11½x10-inch rectangle

2 sides: 8x4½ plus 1-inch roof points

2 long walls: 10x4½-inch rectangles

2 roof halves: 10½x4¾-inch rectangles

1 porch roof: 10½x3-inch rectangle

1 inside chimney top: 2½x2-inch with notch cut for roof

1 inside chimney bottom: 5½x2½-inch rectangle plus point for roof

1 outside chimney: 7¾x2½-inch rectangle

3 recipes Gingerbread Cutouts dough (recipe, page 99)
   Parchment paper and waxed paper
   Disposable decorating bags
   Couplers
1 recipe Royal Icing
   Pretzel sticks and logs
   Cinnamon sticks
   Mixed nuts (about ½ pound)
   Bite-sized shredded wheat biscuits
   Fresh rosemary sprigs
   Gumdrops
   Granulated sugar
1 or 2 recipes Popcorn Trees
1 recipe Almond Trees
   Powdered sugar

Making the Pattern: Make your own pattern pieces, using the dimensions at left. If you'd like to save the paper patterns, cover patterns on both sides with clear adhesive plastic.

Rolling the Dough: Prepare the Gingerbread Cutouts dough; divide into 4 portions. Line countertop with parchment paper. Using a floured rolling pin, roll one portion at a time into a 15×12-inch rectangle (refrigerate remaining dough until needed).

Cutting the Dough: Place patterns ½ inch apart on dough; cut around patterns with a sharp knife. Remove excess dough. Line a large baking sheet with parchment paper. Carefully peel paper from dough cutouts. Arrange dough cutouts on paper-lined baking sheet. To add log texture to front, back, and sides of cabin, press the edge of a ruler or long skewer into the dough, making parallel lines in the dough to resemble stacked logs.

Baking the Pieces: Bake dough cutouts in a 375° oven for 10 to 12 minutes or until edges are brown. While pieces are still very warm, place patterns on cookies and trim excess as necessary. Return cookies to oven about 2 minutes or until firm in center. Carefully

transfer cookies on the parchment paper to a wire rack; cool on rack. Remove cookies from parchment paper. Allow cookies to dry overnight so they become even firmer.

Frosting the Pieces: Fit a decorating bag with a coupler and a medium-size (⅛ inch opening) round tip. Fill bag with Royal Icing. Pipe icing as needed to attach decorations. Decorate front and sides of the cabin as desired, adding pretzel stick above door and pieces of cinnamon stick for window trim. Let decorations dry at least 1 hour before assembling. If decorating tip becomes clogged, wipe with a damp cloth.

Assembling the Walls: Have glass tumblers, glass measuring cups, or coffee mugs handy to hold pieces in place while assembling. On a piece of waxed paper on a display board, set out floor and front, back, and side walls of cabin. Attach sides of cabin to the back piece using a line of Royal Icing where pieces touch. Hold in place using tumblers or mugs (see photo 1, upper right). Pipe icing on the inside of cabin where walls meet floor. Attach front of cabin with icing; hold in place until dry.

Adding the Roof and Chimney: To attach roof, pipe icing along top edges of walls. Gently press the 2 roof pieces into place. To attach chimney, use icing to attach inside chimney bottom to end of cabin. Attach outside chimney piece to inside chimney bottom. Attach inside chimney top to backside of outside chimney piece (see photo 2, middle right). Spread icing onto part of the chimney; cover with nuts. Repeat with icing and nuts until chimney is covered. Frost top of chimney. Set cabin aside to dry.

Building the Porch: Measure and cut 4 pretzel logs to use as supports for the porch roof. Put a dab of Royal Icing on each end of each log. Before the icing dries, attach the porch roof to the front of the cabin with icing. Hold up roof with one hand while setting the pretzel logs in place (see photo 3, below right). Attach logs to porch floor and porch roof.

Tiling the Roof: Spread Royal Icing over bottom half of 1 roof piece. Cover icing with rows of shredded wheat biscuits. Ice and cover top half of roof piece. Repeat on other side.

Finishing Touches: Working on a small area at a time, create icicles on house by spreading dabs of Royal Icing on the roof edge and pulling down with a metal spatula. Make garlands above door and below windows by piping icing above pretzel and cinnamon sticks. Insert small rosemary sprigs into the wet icing. For candlesticks, cut pieces of gumdrops with a sharp knife; mount on window sills. If desired, build pretzel chairs from cut pieces of pretzels glued together with icing.

Setting the Scene: For "snow," sprinkle board with granulated sugar. Arrange Popcorn Trees and Almond Trees around cabin; sift powdered sugar on top.

Building the Fence: Make an "X" shape by using Royal Icing to glue together 2 small pretzel sticks. Repeat to make several "X" shapes. When dry, stabilize the "X"s by standing them in a dish filled with granulated sugar. Lay a pretzel stick across 2 "X"s to make railing; glue with icing. Let dry; place around cabin.

Royal Icing: In a medium bowl, stir together 4½ cups sifted *powdered sugar,* 3 tablespoons *meringue powder,* and ½ teaspoon *cream of tartar.* Add ½ cup *warm water* and 1 teaspoon *vanilla.* Beat with an electric mixer on high speed for 7 to 10 minutes or until extremely stiff. Cover with plastic wrap. Prepared icing may be stored overnight in the refrigerator. To use after storing, beat with an electric mixer until very stiff. *Makes 3 cups.*

1 *Use glass tumblers or coffee mugs to hold the wall pieces in place until the icing dries.*

2 *It's helpful to have someone holding the roof pieces while you glue them. Attaching the chimney right away helps keep the roof together. Next, frost the chimney and decorate with nut "stones."*

3 *To attach the porch, coat both ends of 4 pretzels logs with Royal Icing. Space the logs evenly along the length of the porch. With one hand, hold up the roof and ease the logs in place with your other hand.*

Popcorn Trees: Prepare your favorite popcorn ball recipe; shape mixture into cone shapes to resemble trees.

Almond Trees: For each tree, shape about 2 tablespoons pure *almond paste* (not marzipan) into a cone shape. Starting at the top, press almond slices gently into cone at an angle so that slices point up. Working down, continue adding slices to cover cone.

Ringing In the New Year

While Christmas was celebrated only in varying degrees in early America, the New Year was a holiday for all. Male colonists first celebrated New Year's Eve by drinking, singing, wearing disguises, firing guns, and visiting houses for food and drink. In the late 1700s, the Dutch ladies in New Amsterdam made it a more genteel occasion, opening their parlors on New Year's Day so gentlemen could pay calls on them. And, George Washington received visitors on New Year's Day throughout his presidency at his home in Philadelphia. While many of the foods served at these events simply had party appeal, some had a special symbolic meaning for the New Year. You'll find both in this chapter.

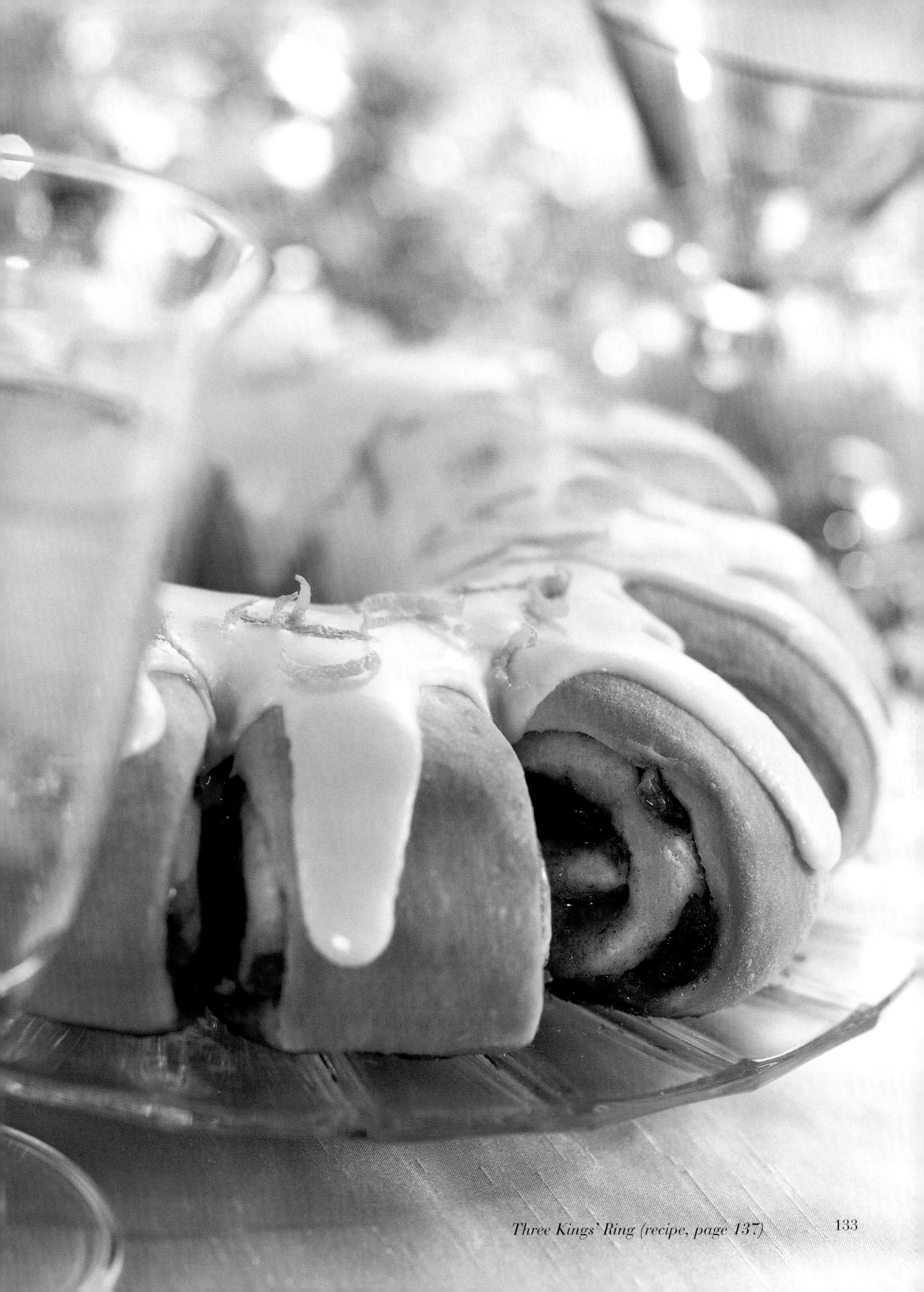

Three Kings' Ring (recipe, page 137)

MENU

New Year's Day Dinner for 8

Whether your goal is good luck, prosperity, good health, or fertility, this menu is bound to bring you something— if you believe the superstitions handed down from our forefathers. At the very least, it'll bring you a great start to the New Year by sharing it with friends and family.

Lentil-Apricot Salad
(recipe right)

Baked ham

Hoppin' John
(recipe opposite)

Turnip Greens with
Bacon (recipe opposite)

Almond Log Cake
(recipe, page 138)

Champagne Peach Punch
(recipe, page 141)

Lentil-Apricot Salad

Prep: 25 minutes • Chill: 1 hour • Stand: 25 minutes

2	cups water or chicken broth
1	cup brown or red lentils
1	clove garlic, minced
4	medium green onions, thinly sliced
1/4	cup snipped fresh mint
1/4	cup extra-virgin olive oil
1/4	cup lemon juice
1/2	teaspoon salt
1/4	teaspoon pepper
1/4	teaspoon ground allspice
1/8	teaspoon ground cinnamon
8	ounces torn spinach (6 cups)
4	ounces dried apricots, thinly sliced (about 2/3 cup)
1/3	cup pistachio nuts

1. In a medium saucepan, combine water, lentils, and garlic. Bring to boiling; reduce heat. Cover and simmer 15 to 20 minutes for brown lentils (3 to 5 minutes for red lentils) or just until lentils are tender. Do not overcook. Drain. Transfer to a medium bowl; set aside.

2. For dressing, in a small bowl, stir together green onions, mint, olive oil, lemon juice, salt, pepper, allspice, and cinnamon. Pour over lentil mixture; toss gently to coat. Cover and refrigerate for at least 1 hour or up to to 8 hours.

3. Before serving, let lentil mixture stand at room temperature for 25 to 30 minutes. Toss with spinach, apricots, and pistachio nuts. *Makes 6 to 8 servings.*

Hoppin' John

Prep: 25 minutes • Cook: 35 minutes • Stand: 10 minutes

8 ounces dry black-eyed peas (1⅓ cups)
½ pound slab bacon, cut into ½-inch cubes
1 medium onion, chopped
4 cups water
½ teaspoon ground red pepper
⅛ teaspoon salt
⅛ teaspoon ground black pepper
¾ cup long grain rice

1. Place black-eyed peas in a colander and rinse with cold water. In a 4½-quart Dutch oven, cook bacon over medium heat until crisp. Drain bacon, reserving *2 tablespoons* drippings in pan. Set bacon aside.

2. Cook onion in the reserved drippings about 5 minutes or until tender.

3. Add black-eyed peas, bacon, water, red pepper, salt, and black pepper to onion. Bring to boiling; reduce heat. Cover and simmer for 20 minutes.

4. Stir in uncooked rice. Return to boiling; reduce heat. Cover and simmer for 15 minutes. Remove from heat; let stand, covered, for 10 minutes. *Makes 8 servings.*

Turnip Greens with Bacon

Prep: 30 minutes • Cook: 1 hour

3 slices bacon, chopped
¼ cup sliced green onions
4 cloves garlic, minced
2 cups water
2 medium turnips, peeled and chopped
(2 cups)
1 cooked smoked pork hock (7 to 8 ounces)
1 tablespoon sugar
¼ teaspoon salt
⅛ to ¼ teaspoon ground red pepper
1 pound turnip greens and/or mustard greens
Red wine vinegar (optional)

1. In a large saucepan, cook bacon over medium heat until crisp. Drain bacon, reserving drippings in saucepan. Set aside.

2. Cook green onions and garlic in the reserved drippings until tender. Carefully add water to green onion mixture. Bring to boiling. Stir in turnips, pork hock, sugar, salt, and red pepper; reduce heat. Cover and simmer for 45 minutes.

3. Meanwhile, wash greens thoroughly in cold water; drain well. Discard stems and any damaged portions. Tear up greens as desired. Add to green onion mixture. Cover and simmer for 15 to 20 minutes or until greens are desired doneness.

4. Remove pork hock. Remove meat from pork hock; chop meat. Return meat to greens mixture; stir in bacon. Heat through. Serve with a slotted spoon. If desired, sprinkle each serving with a little vinegar. *Makes 6 to 8 servings.*

O n New Year's Day, South Carolina cooks serve Hoppin' John, a pea-and-rice dish, with boiled okra and baked yams. Peas are a symbol of fertility according to ancient European beliefs. And planting yams is a fertility ritual in Africa even today.

W hen Southern cooks serve turnip greens or other greens on New Year's Day, the color of money symbolizes prosperity for the coming year. The best season for turnip greens is October through February, so you'll find fresh greens during the holidays.

Pork-Hominy Soup (Posole)

Pork-Hominy Soup (Posole)
Prep: 25 minutes • Cook: 1 hour

1½ pounds lean boneless pork
  2 tablespoons cooking oil
  1 medium onion, chopped
  2 cloves garlic, minced
  4 cups chicken broth
1½ teaspoons dried oregano, crushed
 ¼ teaspoon ground cumin
  2 14½-ounce cans hominy, drained
  1 4-ounce can diced green chile peppers
    Fresh herb sprigs (optional)

1. Trim fat from meat; cut meat into ¾-inch cubes. In a large saucepan or Dutch oven, brown *half* of the meat in hot oil; remove and set aside. Brown remaining meat with onion and garlic. Drain off fat. Return all of the meat to saucepan. Stir in broth, oregano, and cumin. Bring to boiling; reduce heat. Cover; simmer for 40 minutes.

2. Stir in hominy and chile peppers. Cover and simmer for 20 minutes more. Skim off fat. Ladle into soup bowls. If desired, garnish each serving with a sprig of fresh herb. *Makes 6 to 8 servings.*

Fruited Doughnut Balls (Oliebollen)
Prep: 40 minutes • Rise: 30 minutes • Cook: 3 minutes per batch

3¼ cups all-purpose flour
  2 packages active dry yeast
  1 cup milk
  1 cup sugar
 ¼ cup butter
  1 teaspoon salt
  1 teaspoon vanilla
  2 eggs
  3 egg yolks
 ½ cup raisins
 ½ cup diced mixed candied fruits and peels
    Shortening or cooking oil for deep-fat frying
  2 teaspoons ground cinnamon

1. In a large bowl, stir together *2 cups* of the flour and yeast. In a small saucepan, heat and stir milk, *⅓ cup* sugar, butter, and salt just until warm (120° to 130°) and butter is almost melted. Stir in vanilla.

2. Add milk mixture to flour mixture; add eggs and egg yolks. Beat with an electric mixer on low to medium speed for 30 seconds, scraping bowl. Beat on high speed for 3 minutes. Stir in the remaining flour, raisins, and candied fruits and peels. Cover; let rise in a warm place until double in size (about 30 minutes).

3. In a heavy, deep saucepan, heat 3 inches of shortening to 375°. Drop batter by tablespoons, 5 or 6 at a time, into deep hot fat. Fry about 3 minutes or until golden brown, turning once. Drain on paper towels. While still warm, dust with a mixture of *⅔ cup* sugar and the cinnamon. *Makes about 36 oliebollen.*

Three Kings' Ring

Prep: 40 minutes • Rise: 1½ hours • Bake: 25 minutes

3¼ to 3¾ cups all-purpose flour
1 package active dry yeast
⅔ cup milk
⅓ cup granulated sugar
⅓ cup butter
½ teaspoon salt
2 eggs
¼ cup granulated sugar
2 teaspoons ground cinnamon
¾ cup diced candied mixed fruits and peels
½ cup chopped almonds, toasted
3 tablespoons butter, softened
1 recipe Orange Glaze
   Finely shredded orange peel (optional)

1. In a large bowl, stir together *1½ cups* of the flour and the yeast; set aside. In a small saucepan, heat and stir milk, the ⅓ cup granulated sugar, the ⅓ cup butter, and salt just until warm (120° to 130°) and butter is almost melted.

2. Add milk mixture to flour mixture; add eggs. Beat with an electric mixer on low to medium speed for 30 seconds, scraping side of bowl constantly. Beat on high speed for 3 minutes. Using a wooden spoon, stir in as much of the remaining flour as you can.

3. Turn dough out onto a lightly floured surface. Knead in enough of the remaining flour to make a moderately soft dough that is smooth and elastic (3 to 5 minutes total). Shape into a ball. Place dough in a lightly greased bowl, turning once to grease surface. Cover and let rise in a warm place until double in size (1 to 1½ hours).

4. Meanwhile, for filling, in a small bowl, stir together the ¼ cup granulated sugar and cinnamon. Add candied fruits and peels and almonds; toss gently to coat.

5. Punch dough down. Turn out onto a lightly floured surface. Cover and let rest for 10 minutes.

6. Grease a baking sheet; set aside. Roll dough into a 20×12-inch rectangle. Spread with the 3 tablespoons softened butter. Sprinkle with filling. Starting from a long side, loosely roll up into a spiral; moisten edges and seal seam.

7. Place, seam side down, on the prepared baking sheet. Bring ends together to form a ring. Moisten and seal ends. Flatten ring slightly. Using a sharp knife, make 12 cuts around edge of the dough at 1½-inch intervals, cutting about two-thirds of the way to the center. Cover and let rise in a warm place until nearly double in size (30 to 40 minutes).

8. Bake in a 350° oven for 25 to 30 minutes or until bread sounds hollow when lightly tapped. If necessary to prevent overbrowning, cover loosely with foil after 20 minutes of baking. Remove from baking sheet; cool on a wire rack. Spoon Orange Glaze over bread. If desired, sprinkle with orange peel. *Makes 1 ring (12 servings).*

Orange Glaze: In a small bowl, stir together 1 cup sifted *powdered sugar* and ¼ teaspoon *vanilla*. Stir in enough *orange juice* (1 to 2 tablespoons) to make a glaze of drizzling consistency.

Make-Ahead Tip: Prepare, bake, and cool Three Kings' Ring as directed, except do not glaze. Place in a freezer bag. Freeze for up to 3 months. Before serving, thaw at room temperature; spoon Orange Glaze over the bread.

J anuary 6 (Epiphany), or the Twelfth Night, signals the start of Mardi Gras season in New Orleans. Hosts of Twelfth Night parties serve a variation of this breadlike cake with a golden bean hidden inside. Whoever finds the bean becomes the King or Queen of the party, in the long-standing French and Spanish tradition. The person holding the bean also may have to throw the next year's Twelfth Night party. Pictured on page 133.

Almond Log Cake

Prep: 35 minutes • Bake: 12 minutes • Cool: 1 hour

¾ cup sifted cake flour
½ teaspoon ground cinnamon
¼ teaspoon ground nutmeg
5 egg yolks
1 cup granulated sugar
½ cup ground toasted almonds
1 teaspoon vanilla
5 egg whites
⅛ teaspoon salt
⅛ teaspoon cream of tartar
 Powdered sugar
1 recipe Almond Cream Filling
¼ cup sliced almonds, toasted

1. Grease a 15×10×1-inch jelly-roll pan. Line with waxed paper. Grease and flour waxed paper; set aside. In a small bowl, stir together cake flour, cinnamon, and nutmeg; set aside.

2. In a medium bowl, beat egg yolks with an electric mixer on high speed about 5 minutes or until thick and lemon colored. Gradually add granulated sugar, beating on high speed until sugar is nearly dissolved. Stir in ground almonds and vanilla.

3. Thoroughly wash beaters. In a large bowl, beat egg whites, salt, and cream of tartar with an electric mixer on high speed until stiff peaks form (tips stand straight).

4. Fold about *one-fourth* of the beaten egg whites into yolk mixture. Fold yolk mixture into remaining beaten egg whites. Fold in flour mixture just until combined. Spread in the prepared pan.

5. Bake in a 350° oven for 12 to 15 minutes or until cake springs back when lightly touched. Do not allow to brown.

6. Immediately loosen edges of cake from pan. Turn cake out onto a kitchen towel sprinkled with powdered sugar. Remove waxed paper. Roll up warm cake and towel, jelly-roll style, starting from a short side. Cool on a wire rack about 1 hour or until completely cooled.

7. Gently unroll cake. Spread *half* of the Almond Cream Filling onto cake to within 1 inch of the edges. Roll up cake without towel. Place on a serving platter.

8. Frost cake with remaining filling. Serve immediately or refrigerate for up to 8 hours before serving. Sprinkle with toasted sliced almonds. *Makes 12 servings.*

Almond Cream Filling: In a large bowl, beat 1¾ cups *whipping cream* on medium speed until soft peaks form (tips curl); set aside. Finely crumble one 8-ounce can *almond paste* into another large bowl. Add ¼ cup *whipping cream* and 2 tablespoons *amaretto* or 2 teaspoons *vanilla*. Beat on low speed until nearly smooth. Fold about *one-fourth* of the whipped cream into almond paste mixture to lighten. Fold remaining whipped cream into almond paste mixture. *Makes about 4 cups.*

A log cake sweetly celebrates the French custom of burning a Yule log to prevent bad spirits from flowing down the chimney into the new year. Fortuitous almonds, another coin symbol, add extra value.

Honey Pistachio Tart
Prep: 50 minutes • Bake: 35 minutes

½ cup granulated sugar
¼ cup honey
¼ cup water
1½ cups chopped pistachio nuts, toasted
½ cup snipped dried apricots, chopped
    crystallized ginger, and/or golden raisins
¼ cup milk
1 tablespoon butter or margarine
1 recipe Rich Orange Pastry
1 slightly beaten egg yolk
  Coarse sugar

1. For filling, in a small saucepan, stir together granulated sugar, honey, and water. Bring to boiling, stirring until sugar is dissolved. Reduce heat to medium-low. Cook about 15 minutes or until mixture is a light caramel color, stirring occasionally.

2. Stir in nuts, apricots, milk, and butter. Return to boiling; reduce heat. Simmer, uncovered, about 5 minutes or until slightly thickened, stirring occasionally. Set aside.

3. Meanwhile, on a lightly floured surface, roll *one portion* of the Rich Orange Pastry into a 16×6-inch rectangle. Carefully transfer to a 13½×4-inch rectangular tart pan with a removable bottom. Press pastry into fluted sides; trim edges. Top with filling.

4. Roll remaining pastry into 10-inch square. Using fluted pastry wheel, cut into ½-inch-wide strips. Weave strips diagonally on filling to create a lattice, pressing ends onto rim of pan. Brush with egg yolk; sprinkle with coarse sugar.

5. Bake in a 375° oven about 35 minutes or until top is golden. (If parts of crust brown too quickly, cover with foil.) Cool in pan on a wire rack. Remove side of pan. Transfer to a serving platter. *Makes 8 to 12 servings.*

Rich Orange Pastry: In a large bowl, stir together 2 cups *all-purpose flour* and 2 teaspoons finely shredded *orange peel*. Using a pastry blender, cut in ⅔ cup *butter* until pieces are pea-size. In a small bowl, stir together 1 beaten *egg* and ¼ cup *cold water*. Gradually stir egg mixture into flour mixture just until moistened. Divide in half. Form each half into a ball.

Caraway Cookies
Prep: 25 minutes • Chill: 3 hours • Bake: 7 minutes per batch

2 cups all-purpose flour
1 tablespoon caraway seed
1 teaspoon baking powder
¼ teaspoon baking soda
¼ teaspoon salt
½ cup butter
1 cup sugar
2 eggs

1. In a medium bowl, stir together flour, caraway seed, baking powder, baking soda, and salt; set aside.

2. In a large bowl, beat butter with an electric mixer on medium to high speed for 30 seconds. Add sugar. Beat until combined, scraping side of bowl. Beat in eggs, one at a time, beating well after each addition. Beat in as much of the flour mixture as you can with the mixer. Using a wooden spoon, stir in any remaining flour mixture. Divide dough in half. Cover and refrigerate about 3 hours or until easy to handle.

3. Lightly grease a cookie sheet; set aside. On a lightly floured surface, roll dough, *half* at a time, to ⅛ inch thickness. Cut with 2½-inch cookie cutters. Place 2 inches apart on prepared cookie sheet. Bake in a 375° oven for 7 to 8 minutes or until edges are light brown. Remove from cookie sheet; cool on a wire rack. *Makes about 54 cookies.*

Jewish families celebrate their New Year at Rosh Hashana in September instead of in January. They often serve foods with honey and fruit in them. Honey symbolizes hope for a sweet new year, and fruit suggests the bounty of the harvest.

Caraway Cookies

These caraway-spiced cookies were called New Year's Cakes by the Dutch cooks who served them at their New Year's Day open houses in New Amsterdam.

oasting the New Year and everyone's good health is what the holiday is all about, from watching the ball drop in New York's Times Square to lighting bonfires in the South. Since New Year's open houses started back in the 1700s, hosts have been setting out punches, hot toddies, wine, cordials, and liqueurs on the sideboard, ready for well-wishers to stop by.

Clockwise from front: Hot Cranberry Toddy, Champagne Peach Punch, and Orange Mint Juleps

Hot Cranberry Toddy
Start to finish: 20 minutes

- 1 48-ounce bottle (6 cups) cranberry juice
- 2 cups water
- ½ cup sugar
- ¼ cup lemon juice
- 3 1-inch-long strips lemon peel
- 3 inches stick cinnamon
- 1 teaspoon whole cloves
- ⅓ cup bourbon, rum, or orange juice

1. In a 4-quart saucepan or Dutch oven, combine cranberry juice, water, sugar, and lemon juice.

2. For spice bag, place lemon peel, cinnamon, and cloves in the center of a double-thick, 6-inch square of 100%-cotton cheesecloth. Bring the corners together; tie with a clean string. Add to juice mixture.

3. Bring just to boiling; reduce heat. Cover and simmer for 10 minutes. Discard spice bag. Stir bourbon into cranberry mixture. Transfer to a heatproof serving carafe or pot. Garnish as desired. *Makes 12 servings.*

Champagne Peach Punch
Start to finish: 20 minutes

- 1 16-ounce package frozen unsweetened peach slices
- ¼ cup sugar
- 2½ cups orange juice
- 2 tablespoons lemon juice or lime juice
- 1 750-milliliter bottle champagne or sparkling wine or 4 cups unsweetened pineapple juice
- Cubed or crushed ice

1. Thaw peaches at room temperature, but do not drain.

2. In a blender container or food processor bowl, combine peaches, their juice, and sugar. Cover and blend or process until smooth.

3. Transfer pureed peaches to a 2-quart pitcher. Stir in orange juice and lemon juice. Before serving, slowly pour in champagne, stirring with an up-and-down motion. Serve over ice. If desired, garnish with additional peach slices. *Makes about 12 servings.*

Make-Ahead Tip: After stirring in orange and lemon juices, cover and refrigerate overnight or until serving time.

Orange Mint Juleps
Prep: 20 minutes • Stand: 1 hour

- 2 cups water
- ⅔ cup sugar
- 1 cup snipped fresh mint
- 1 teaspoon finely shredded orange peel
- 2 cups orange juice
- ⅔ cup lemon juice
- ⅓ cup bourbon or vodka (optional)
- Cracked ice
- Fresh mint (optional)

1. In a medium saucepan, combine water and sugar. Bring to boiling, stirring until sugar is dissolved. Pour over snipped mint. Stir in orange peel, orange juice, and lemon juice. Cover and let stand at room temperature for 1 hour.

2. Pour through a strainer into a pitcher; discard solids. If desired, stir bourbon into juice mixture. Cover and refrigerate for up to 24 hours. Serve over ice. If desired, garnish with fresh mint. *Makes 8 servings.*

Hot toddies take the edge off a chilly January day. These steaming drinks simmer with fruit, spices, and usually some form of alcohol. All-American cranberries and bourbon fortify this version, although orange juice could be substituted for the alcohol.

Champagne is perhaps the most widely served beverage at New Year's parties today, with a toast right at midnight and a refrain of "Auld Lang Syne." The champagne always used to come from France, but now many revelers share their toast with a glass of California's own sparkling wine.

Our American Christmas Traditions

Amidst the excitement of the holiday season and the spicy scents of evergreens and gingerbread cookies, it's easy to forget that the Christmas we know today is a relatively recent American holiday. Although Europeans have celebrated Christmas in the Old World for hundreds of years, our Puritan ancestors rejected these "pagan" excesses. Appalled by the drinking and rollicking that arose at the end of each harvest season, they dismissed the excuse

Pear and Mincemeat Tart, page 27

that hardworking laborers deserved a rowdy respite from the intense routine—a last splurge before work began again in the spring. Many of the colonies banned any public observance on December 25—enacting laws that stayed on the books until 1856 in Massachusetts and until 1861 in New Hampshire! So, for the Puritans, Christmas Day was business as usual. They attended church, then went about their daily tasks. Martha Ballard, an 18th-century Maine midwife, chronicled the many babies she delivered on or around Christmas Day, but she also noted baking mincemeat pies on December 25 to give to friends and family.

Other groups and regions in the New World welcomed the holiday as an opportunity to visit family and friends and to load their tables with the abundance of the new land. When George Washington married the widow Martha Custis during the Christmas season of 1759, their lavish wedding feast included spit-roasted sides of beef and pork, succulent country hams, an amazing array of jellies, jams, molded desserts, fruitcakes, pies, eggnog, punch, and Mrs. Washington's own recipe for "Rich, Black Great Cake."

In 1778, frontiersmen along the Kentucky border celebrated the holiday with wild turkey, venison, bear, rabbit, and the *piéce de résistance*—a huge possum, baked whole and suspended over the table!

Apricot-Cherry Fruitcake, page 78

In 18th-century Williamsburg, December meant that larders were full from the harvest and that meat was plentiful. Ham, beef, mutton, turkey, goose—along with oysters and crabs—were all ready for a feast. The tables of more prosperous families were laden with such exotics as sugared almonds and walnuts, crystallized flower petals, marzipan, and candied ginger.

On his plantation in Westover, Virginia, William Byrd II noted in his diary that on Christmas Day he ate turkey for breakfast, visited friends, went to church, then dined on wild goose, boiled pigeon, venison, minced mutton, and other delicacies.

The 1800s brought waves of immigrants to the United States, carrying with them their homelands' holiday customs—in particular their treasured recipes for Christmas foods. What began as European breads, cookies, cakes, and pies took on new flavors as these cooks added inspired touches of American ingenuity and imagination. They were surprised, delighted, and challenged by the varied and sometimes unfamiliar foods available to them: pumpkins, corn, and popcorn; wild turkey and other game; maple sugar and

Roast Stuffed Turkey with Cranberry-Pecan Stuffing, pages 15 and 17

and honey; oysters, crabs, trout, and other freshwater fish; new varieties of peaches, apples, and other fruits; and a plentiful supply of wild nuts and berries, especially cranberries. These all found a permanent place in a burgeoning

Steamed Cranberry Pudding, page 26

unique American cuisine. Steamed cranberry pudding graced the holiday table beside traditional plum pudding. Housewives found innumerable ways to prepare the abundant corn crops—Indian pudding became a family favorite. Pumpkin pies appeared in all guises, and cooks took pride in their signature mincemeat recipes.

American attitudes toward the celebration of Christmas gradually changed in the 19th century, and by the 1850s, Christmas had become a family-oriented holiday, a festival primarily for children. Modest gifts of oranges or candy were stuffed into children's Christmas stockings. Evergreen Christmas trees, first introduced by German immigrants, grew in popularity and in size. Families strung strands of cranberries and popcorn and baked cookie ornaments to adorn these beloved symbols of the season.

In the South, holiday hospitality was lavish, with large, extravagant Christmas meals shared by friends and families. The 19th-century cookbook author Marian Harland remembered Christmas Eve suppers in Virginia that included waffles, ham, beaten biscuits, honey, and three kinds of preserves. Christmas dinner brought the traditional roast pig—the whitest and plumpest the market could offer, buttered "from nose to toes" and coated with bread crumbs. Christmas night was devoted to stirring a molasses stew for a taffy pull, so children and adults alike could stretch the sticky mixture into shining ribbons and braids.

Christmas in the South also was a time for grand parties and balls. Sumptuous refreshment tables were laden with oysters, country ham, sweet potato pie, Kentucky bourbon cake, coconut cake, and pecan pie. The slaves were remembered by more generous masters, who provided barbecued hogs and steers, apple dumplings, dried peaches, and liquor, which was forbidden during the rest of the year.

Sweet Potato Pie, page 28

The onset of the Civil War brought a new meaning to Christmas. In her 1867 classic, *Little Women,* Louisa May Alcott described Christmas in the March family household during the austere days of the war. Jo, Beth, Meg, and Amy looked forward to their holiday breakfast of muffins, griddle cakes, and cream, but their mother suggested they give it to a poor family. "I think there were not in all the city four merrier people than the four girls who gave away their breakfasts and contented themselves with bread and milk on Christmas morning," wrote Alcott.

Apple Griddle Cakes, page 52

After the war ended, Americans began moving west and south again, once more bundling up their recipes and adapting them to whatever ingredients they'd find along the way. Regional specialties developed, and the diversity of American cooking became increasingly apparent.

Settlers on the prairies and plains found that rural Christmas celebrations were far less sophisticated than those they'd enjoyed in eastern cities. Fuel for household ovens on the prairie was scarce, and Christmas cookies frequently were baked in "grassburner" ovens, stoked with bundles of dried prairie grass.

1874

Frontier women adapted recipes brought from home, often without the familiar ingredients they previously had deemed necessary. When Martha Summerhayes, the wife of a dashing young Army lieutenant, followed him from New England into Arizona Territory in 1874, their first home at Camp Mohave was a simple tent set in the desert, with neither a tree nor a bush to provide shade. Her husband suggested she make some of the wonderful Nantucket doughnuts he remembered. When she asked feebly where she could get eggs, he replied, "Oh, we have no eggs. You're on the frontier now and must learn to do without eggs."

Pork-Hominy Soup (Posole), page 136

Living in the Southwest, Martha would have found that beans, hominy, chile peppers, corn, and tortillas supplied daily needs, but during the Christmas season, *buñuelos,* a deep-fried cinnamon-sugar bread, was a Southwest version of her beloved doughnut. The tradition of the piñata still provides party guests the opportunity to bang away with a stick at light pottery or paper representations of a man, clown, bird, or donkey. When the piñata breaks, everyone scambles to pick up the cookies, candies, and toys that spill out.

Another frontier bride found herself in Wyoming, in isolated ranching country. In a generous and courageous moment, Elinore Pruitt Stewart decided to make Christmas special for the sheepherders who spent long winter months tending their animals in virtual exile from civilization. She and a friend roasted geese and

Anadama Bread, page 63

ham, packed boxes with their best rye bread, a tub of doughnuts, iced coffee cakes, and 13 pounds of butter, then drove a sleigh through high drifts of snow to deliver their heartfelt gifts to the surprised and delighted men.

The Scandinavian families who settled in the Midwest also thought nothing of traveling long distances on foot or in wagons in snowy weather. They would gather to cook and eat enormous meals based on traditional dishes, some with an American twist. *Lutefisk* (Norwegian cod steeped in white lye) and *lefse* (potato pancakes) joined scalloped corn, carrots, hazelnut meringue cakes, and dozens of tender butter cookies.

Also in the Midwest, but in the East as well, Pennsylvania Dutch cooks perfected dozens of Christmas specialties, such as cookies made with handcrafted cookie cutters in many shapes and sizes. The well-known German *lebkuchen,* or gingerbread, took on a new American personality when cooks added lemon, coconuts, raisins, and even gum drops to the old recipes. Pennsylvania Dutch housewives also developed their own mincemeat, made with green tomatoes, for tarts and pies.

Moravian Christmas Cookies, page 102

Pennsylvania also was home to the Moravians who celebrated Christmas with their traditional Old World Love Feast. Sugar cake, Christmas cookies, love feast buns, and special candlelight church services still mark the occasion in Bethlehem, Pennsylvania, and Old Salem, North Carolina.

By 1890, food had become a focal point of the holiday. Cookbooks and magazines, such as *Godey's Lady's Book* touted lavish menus and recipes. *Successful Farming* magazine, first published in 1902, began featuring recipes for farm wives. While children eagerly pored over mail-order catalogs, the aroma of homemade candy—fondants, chocolate drops, taffy, and coconut creams—drifted from the kitchen. Almost everything was homemade—Christmas breads, pickles, pear jam, biscuits, mashed potatoes, roast chicken, and fruit cake.

Christmas Menu
Godey's Lady's Book, 1890

Raw Oysters.....Bouillon
Fried Smelts.....Sauce Tartare
Potatoes a la Maitre d'Hotel
Sweetbread Patés.....Peas
Roast Turkey.....Cranberry Sauce
Roman Punch
Quail with Truffles.....Rice Croquettes
Parisian Salad
Crackers and Cheese
Nesselrode Pudding.....Fancy Cakes
Fruit
Coffee

Throughout the years, the tradition of caroling continued in many forms, but always with warm refreshment in mind, just as in the early colonial days. In the cities, merry bands trooped from house to house, gathering for a party at the end of the singing. In the country, families would bundle up in the sleigh or car to visit the neighbors for carol singing and a sumptuous potluck. In 1912, a group of young people on Boston's Beacon Hill began the tradition of bell ringing, ending their evening with an elaborate buffet of Christmas treats. Those bells turned out to be tolling for a war that would take many American men and women to foreign shores where they'd be fighting for liberties their forefathers had embraced in America.

When World War I ended, men returned to start families, setting up their homes in neighborhoods near the city centers, beginning a shift from rural to suburban living. These new families were looking for ways to enrich their lives. So in 1922, when *Better Homes and Gardens*® magazine published its first issue, it touched people where they lived—at home with their families. The magazine began its tradition of offering holiday recipes every year, just like the recipes featured in this cookbook today.

To help families keep track of all of their favorite family recipes, the *Better Homes and Gardens Cookbook* first was published in 1930, with a ring binding so readers could add their own family recipes. The familiar red plaid cover later was wrapped around the cookbook that eventually would wind up in more than 30 million homes, outsold by only the bible and the dictionary.

Caramel-Nut Corn, page 124

Cooking at home became more practical as the economic constraints of the Great Depression became routine in the 1930s. But even in times of crisis, Americans have managed to celebrate Christmas. During those lean years, *Better Homes and Gardens* magazine encouraged housewives to find imaginative ways to stretch food budgets—creating eggless cakes and apple pies without apples and trimming trees with homemade ornaments, popcorn, and cookies.

The outbreak of World War II brought more challenges for American cooks. Despite food rationing, mothers managed to send boxes of cookies and candies to their boys overseas, so magazines and cookbooks offered sturdy cookie recipes for shipping. The military also provided special holiday meals to the men as a respite from the daily GI fare. In 1944, a Marine sergeant recovering from wounds aboard a hospital ship wrote home that he and his friends were served "white and dark tom turkey meat, giblet gravy, cranberry sauce, pickles, olives, plum pudding, fruitcake, and iced tea. Soon our eyes no longer bulged, our stomachs did. It was a strange, almost unbelievable sight to see us, so grotesque in our bandages and casts, all so thankful to be among the living."

Today, the delicious smells and tastes of Christmas call to mind the holidays of our childhoods. We bake the cookies our mothers baked, the breads our grandmothers passed along, and each time we try a new Christmas recipe, we shape our own traditions. While we're in the kitchen together, we share our memories with our parents, grandparents, aunts, and uncles and our own children, each of us creating our version of an American Christmas.

Cookie Assortment, pages 96–97

The recipes and memories may change over the years, but what doesn't change is the American spirit of giving. This year, as you make lists of who will receive your homemade goodies, plan to bake an extra dozen cookies for a nursing home or a cake for a homeless shelter. Food nourishes the spirit as well as the body, and a gift from your kitchen really is a gift from your heart. That's what Christmas in America is all about.

Our American Holiday Table

Like most American traditions, our holiday table settings come from a melting pot of customs. Ancient Egyptians decorated their celebrative dishes with exotic flowers. Tabletops in early Renaissance paintings depict the use of knives, colorful plates, and goblets, along with decorative table coverings in varying lengths. Seventeenth- and eighteenth-century art introduced spoons, candelabras, covered dishes, and napkins. The nineteenth century ushered in an array of ornate flatware, handcut crystal glassware, and museum-quality porcelain. To see how you can adapt these ideas for your all-American table, turn the page.

Ribbon Wrap-up

Ribbons were first introduced to the American tabletop as a colorful, inexpensive substitute for napkin rings and as a garnish for flower arrangements. Party hosts also used ribbons to decorate Christmas sweets and party favors. Today, ribbons tie it all together. On the left, a ribbon-wrapped fruit bowl and salad plate indicates the meal is a gift to each guest. Sheer golden fabric adds inviting texture and holiday cheer to a simple stack of plates. Ribbons are ideal on tables where decorating space is limited; use two or three in one or more colors as a free-flowing connection between serving dishes.

Berry Embellishment

Fresh seasonal greens became a part of most American Christmas table settings in the 1850s, shortly after the Christmas tree was adopted. Branches trimmed from the trees still add color to American mantels and tabletops today. Holly was also very popular in the nineteenth century; its sharp pointed leaves were said to ward off evil spirits. Santa was often seen wearing a sprig in his hat. Because it remains glossy and green in winter, holly has symbolized life and warm wishes of good health. As pictured right, use holly and other greens with colorful berries to adorn napkins, flower arrangements, and candleholders. But, be careful not to use holly or its berries to garnish food, as it is toxic.

Present Place Holder

Place cards became a part of the American tabletop to facilitate seating parties of eight or more guests. Tradition calls for the card to be placed on a napkin (across the service plate) as shown, or in a convenient spot at the top of the setting in a decorative holder. In the late 1800s, Christmas ornaments began to serve as party favors for guests. Today, as pictured left, you can combine the two traditions to add a personal touch to your table and to offer souvenirs of a special dinner.

Firelight

Imaginative table settings were as big a hit in colonial times as they are today. On the right, a row of pear candles serves as a narrow centerpiece for the colonial-style table, creating a soft silhouette of firelight and an inviting ambience. A wooden tray protects the tabletop from wax drippings. A knife and fork laid across mismatched plates add a nostalgic touch to the setting, harking back to days gone by. Napkins draped under the plates give the impression of a tablecloth, even though the table has been purposely left uncovered.

153

Button Beauty

Throughout American history, hard times have called for inexpensive, creative decorating, both on and off the table. In the colonial days, old buttons sewn to white linens added color for very little money. For extra glamour on today's table, choose vintage buttons in colors to complement the table linens, as on the left. The eclectic theme carries over to a colorful table linen topped with plain white vintage plates.

Botanical Bliss

Early in American history, fresh flowers during the winter months were scarce and expensive commodities. In the 1830s, select greenhouses began carrying poinsettias, but it was not until the 1870s that New York florists began selling them at Christmas time. Seasonal greenery was the botanical embellishment of choice and remains nearly as popular today. A long-lasting arrangement of white blossoms and green foliage adds a sophisticated touch to the table on the right.

Party Favor

Holiday giving is a custom that dates back to ancient times. The Bible describes presents given to the Christ child from the wise men to celebrate His birth. In America, gift-giving dates to the 1700s, when Dutch immigrants looked to Saint Nicholas to bring them small treats. By the early 1800s, family gift exchanges were prevalent and remain so today. For a festive holiday feast, set small gift-wrapped boxes at each place setting, as on the left, to add color to the table and excitement to the air.

Fruitful Fun

Both fresh and canned fruits were favorite gifts of colonial Americans. Apples kept in the cellar lasted for months and could be shared with neighbors and friends; fresh pears had a shorter season, and could be enjoyed only until the end of the harvest. On the right, a tasty pear serves a dual purpose as both a first course and a place-card holder. To create the same effect, slit one side of the fruit. For added stability, cut a flat slice off the bottom or prop the edible place holder against a fruit or soup bowl placed on your plate.

155

Soft Silhouette

Ornate candelabras began adding light and glitter to banquet tables during the seventeenth century. Their flattering glow makes both food and guests look their best, which may be why their popularity continues today. Until the 1970s, American etiquette books suggested that tabletop candlesticks be used only after dusk, but now we use candles to add a cozy touch any time. To hold the candles, you can use candlesticks, votives, or trays, as on the left. To prevent flickering in guests' eyes, position each candle high or low enough so when guests are seated, the flame is above or below eye level. One candle per guest is not overdoing it; however, fewer candles can look equally attractive.

Personal Touch

As in home decorating, the biggest trend in the American holiday tabletop is personalization. Choose ornamentation that says something about you and your family. If you love gardening, adorn your table with a pot of your favorite flowers, as on the right. If you like to grow your own vegetables, create a funky arrangement with mini pumpkins or squash or other colorful edibles. Choose colors that complement your decor; red and green are no longer the only colors of the season. Golds, silvers, whites, and other neutrals, as well as blues, peaches, and plums, are all gaining in popularity and can be used to create a setting that makes a statement about you.

Note: The illustration on page 143 is courtesy of Winterthur Library: Joseph Downs Collection of Manuscripts and Printed Ephemera, No. Col. 308.